Contents

What you need to know about the National Tests	ii
Preparing and practising for the English Test	iv

Paper 1	Reading and Writing (Levels 4–7)	1
Paper 2	Shakespeare (Levels 4–7)	5
Answers to Papers 1 and 2		9
How to approach Paper 1		9
How to mark Paper 1		15
How to approach Paper 2		28
How to mark Paper 2		32
Determining your level for Papers 1 and 2		46

Grammar section	47
Answers to the Grammar section	55
Determining your level for the Grammar section	59

English Booklet

What you need to know about the National Tests

KEY STAGE 3 NATIONAL TESTS: HOW THEY WORK

Students between the ages of 11 and 14 (Years 7–9) cover Key Stage 3 of the National Curriculum. In May of their final year of Key Stage 3 (Year 9), all students take written National Tests (commonly known as SATs) in English, Mathematics and Science. The tests are carried out in school, under the supervision of teachers, but are marked by examiners outside the school.

The tests help to show what you have learned in these key subjects. They also help parents and teachers to know whether students are reaching the standards set out in the National Curriculum. The results may be used by your teacher to help place you in the appropriate teaching group for some of your GCSE courses.

You will probably spend around seven hours in total sitting the tests during one week in May. Most students will do two test papers in each of English, Maths and Science.

The school sends the papers away to external examiners for marking. The school will then report the results of the tests to you and your parents by the end of July, along with the results of assessments made by teachers in the classroom, based on your work throughout Key Stage 3. You will also receive a summary of the results for all students at the school, and for students nationally. This will help you to compare your performance with that of other students of the same age. The report from your school will explain to you what the results show about your progress, strengths, particular achievements and targets for development. It may also explain how to follow up the results with your teachers.

UNDERSTANDING YOUR LEVEL OF ACHIEVEMENT

The National Curriculum divides standards for performance in each subject into a number of levels, from one to eight. On average, students are expected to advance one level for every two years they are at school. By Year 9 (the end of Key Stage 3), you should be at Level 5 or 6. The table on page iii shows how you are expected to progress through the levels at ages 7, 11 and 14 (the end of Key Stages 1, 2 and 3).

For English, there are two test papers: Paper 1 assesses Reading and Writing and Paper 2 assesses your understanding of and personal response to extracts from a Shakespeare play. Paper 1 will be $1\frac{3}{4}$ hours long and Paper 2 will be $1\frac{1}{4}$ hours long. An extension paper with high level questions is also available for exceptionally able students.

More emphasis is being placed on grammar, spelling and punctuation. The Grammar section in this book will help you to achieve better marks in Papers 1 and 2. It will also help you to answer separate grammar questions.

What you need to know about the National Tests

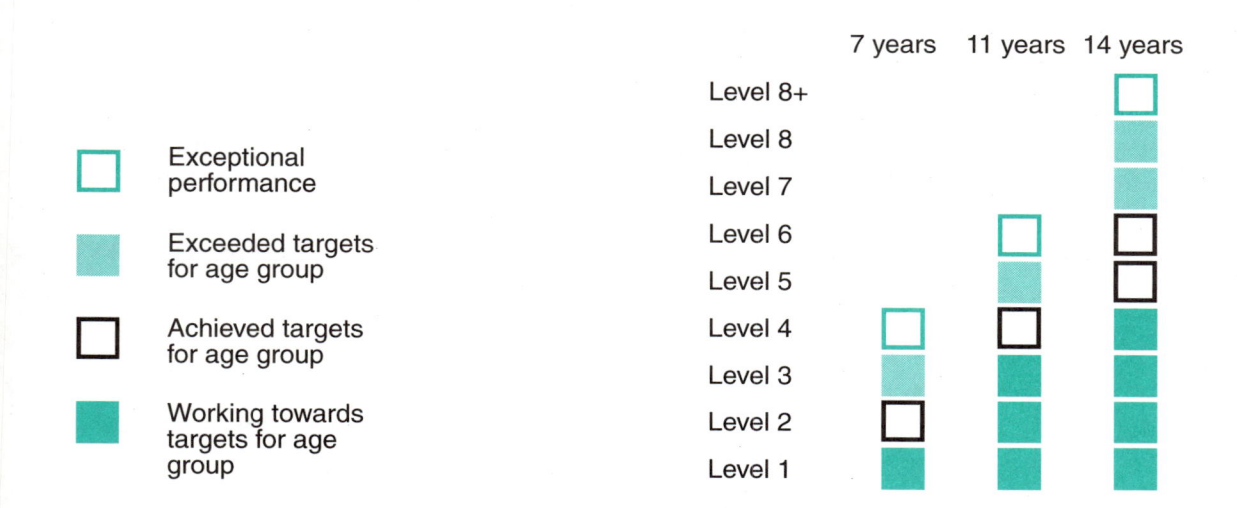

How you should progress

- Exceptional performance
- Exceeded targets for age group
- Achieved targets for age group
- Working towards targets for age group

This book concentrates on Levels 4–7, providing two test papers with plenty of questions to practise plus an additional Grammar section. The bar chart below shows you what percentage of students nationally reached each of the levels in the 1999 tests for English.

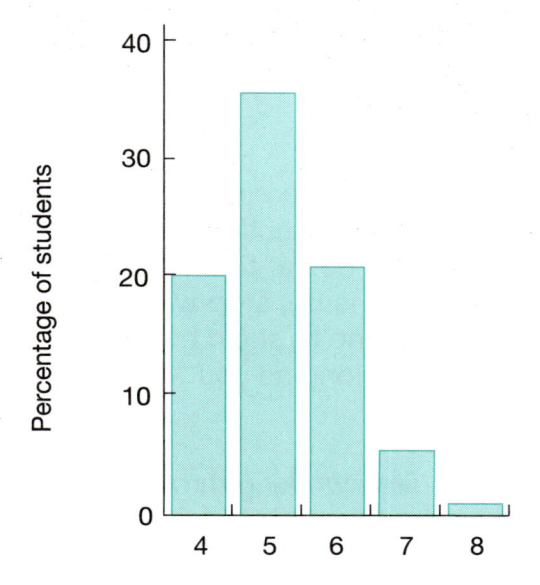

Levels achieved in English, 1999

Preparing and practising for the English Test

ENGLISH AT KEY STAGE 3
The questions in this book will test you on the Key Stage 3 curriculum for English. For assessment purposes, the National Curriculum divides English into three sections, called Attainment Targets (ATs). The first AT, Speaking and Listening, is assessed only by the teacher in the classroom, not in the written tests. The other two ATs are Reading and Writing. The National Curriculum describes levels of performance for each of the English ATs. These AT levels are taken together to give an overall level for English. The test papers assess both Reading and Writing.

USING THIS BOOK TO HELP YOU PREPARE
This book contains four basic features:

Questions:	one Reading and Writing paper and one Shakespeare paper for Levels 4–7, plus an additional Grammar section
Answers:	showing you how to approach each question, and how to mark your answers using assessment criteria and model answers
Examiner's Tips:	giving advice on how to improve your answers
Level Charts:	showing you how to interpret your marks to arrive at a level

PAPER 1 (READING AND WRITING)
The test questions are based on the passages in the English booklet at the back of this book, which can be detached. Try Paper 1 first. Before you begin, read through the paper. Then turn to the Answers section and read through the guidance on how to approach Paper 1 in general, and how to approach each question in turn.

Carry out the test in a place where you are comfortable. You will need a pen and some lined writing paper. Read the instructions for Paper 1 carefully before you begin. Note the starting time in the box at the top of the test and time yourself during the test. When the test time is up, stop writing. If you have not finished, but wish to continue working, draw a line to show how much you completed within the test time. Then continue for as long as you wish, but do not count the 'extra' writing when you mark the paper.

Mark your answers to Paper 1 first, working through the model answers and advice. Enter your marks on the Marking Grid on page 46 and look at the Level Chart to determine your level for Paper 1.

PAPER 2 (SHAKESPEARE)
Carry out Paper 2 on a different day. Three Shakespeare extracts are reproduced in the English booklet, at the back of this book. Answer one question on the play you have studied in school. Regardless of which scenes are chosen for the actual test, you will be expected to know the entire play. This book includes scenes for

Preparing and practising for the English Test

each play, enabling you to practise the skills involved in answering questions about the play you know best.

Again, review how to approach Paper 2 and the question for your chosen play in the Answers section before you attempt your own answer. Answer and mark Paper 2 in the same way as Paper 1.

MARKING PAPERS 1 AND 2

When you have finished a test, turn to the section on how to mark your paper in the Answers section. Read the assessment criteria for each question, as well as the model answer, which has been marked for you. The model answers are of a very high quality and are intended to help you focus your revision. When you are judging your own answers, remember that an answer does not have to be perfect to score high marks.

It is very difficult for anyone to mark his or her own writing. When using this book, you may want to ask a parent or friend to help you judge your answers. Use the assessment criteria to award yourself the appropriate number of marks for each question. Write your score in the top half of the mark boxes on the test. Enter the marks you scored for each question on the Marking Grid on page 46. Then add them up to find the total for the test. Look at the Level Charts on page 46 to determine your level for each paper, as well as an overall level for Papers 1 and 2 combined.

GRAMMAR SECTION (SPELLING, PUNCTUATION AND GRAMMAR)

The marking schemes for Papers 1 and 2 already include consideration of your abilities to apply your knowledge of these elements of English.

However, in response to the demand for more emphasis to be placed on grammar, there is an extra section on grammar on pages 47–59. Working through this section will improve your ability in this important aspect of English. It will also help to improve your marks for Papers 1 and 2.

MARKING THE GRAMMAR SECTION

You will find the answers for this section on pages 55–59. Ask a parent, friend or teacher to help you mark your answers. Spelling is easy to mark because it is either right or wrong but the other questions may have alternative answers that are also correct. Use the Marking Grid on page 59 to find out how well you have done.

Preparing and practising for the English Test

FINALLY, AS THE TESTS DRAW NEAR
In the days before the tests, make sure you are as relaxed and confident as possible. You can help yourself by:

- ensuring you know what test papers you will be doing;

- working through practice questions, and improving your answers.

Above all, don't worry too much! Although the National Tests do matter, your achievements throughout the school year are more important and will underpin your performance in these tests. Do your best; that is all anyone can ask.

Paper 1
Reading and Writing

PAPER 1
LEVELS 4–7

Instructions to student

- Carefully detach pages 1–14 from the back of this book. Fasten the pages together to make your own English booklet. Paper 1 is based on pages 1–4 of this booklet.

- First of all, you have 15 minutes to read the paper. You may make notes and annotate the passages in the booklet. Do not start to write your answers until the 15 minutes of reading time are over.

- You then have 1 hour 30 minutes to write your answers.

- Answer **all** of the questions in Sections A and B, and **one** question only from Section C.

- You should spend about:
    - 10 minutes on Question 1
    - 20 minutes on Question 2
    - 20 minutes on Question 3
    - 40 minutes on Question 4

    Your spelling and handwriting will be assessed on Section C of this paper. Check your work carefully.

This English test does not demand a particular number of words per question.

Taking this practice paper will show you how much you are able to write under timed conditions.

Look at the marks available for each question. This is shown in the box in the margin, for example,

15

In the 15 minutes of reading time, you should first skim read in order to get a sense of the whole paper. Then read the passages, questions and assignments more carefully.

Remember, effective reading and writing is dependent on **thinking** and (within the limits of a test situation) **planning**.

Paper 1

Start ☐ **Finish** ☐

Section A

Read the passage **Talking in Whispers** *which is on pages 1–2 of the English booklet.*

Then answer Question 1 and Question 2.

1 The first 61 lines describe what Andres sees and does.

> **How does the writer show the reader what is happening and how Andres is involved?**

In your answer you should comment on:
- the way the writer uses physical details;
- how Andres' reactions and feelings change;
- what Andres thinks and feels.

Refer to words or phrases from the passage to support your ideas.

2 Read the rest of the passage from line 62 to the end.

> **How effectively do you think this section builds up a picture of increasing danger yet gives hope of Andres doing something about the violence?**

In your answer you should comment on:
- how the writer uses details of the soldier's violence;
- the American photographer, his role and importance;
- the behaviour of the soldiers.

Refer to words and phrases from this section of the extract to support your ideas.

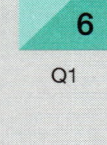

Paper 1

Section B

Read the two pages from Oxfam's internet site, reproduced on pages 3-4 of the English booklet. These pages are intended to promote Oxfam's campaign for children's worldwide right to education.

Now answer Question 3.

3

> **The web pages are designed to interest and involve people in Oxfam's Education Now! campaign. How do the pages do this?**

In your answer you should comment on:

- the information given;
- the language used;
- the way words, layout and images are used.

Paper 1

Section C

This section is a test of writing. You will be assessed on:
- *your ideas and the way you organise and express them;*
- *your ability to write clearly, using paragraphs and accurate grammar, spelling and punctuation.*

Choose **ONE** of the following:

4 EITHER

a

> **Write about a threatening situation. You could write about a real or imaginary event. Try to build up a feeling of tension or suspense.**

> ### Examiner's tip
> In your answer you could include:
> - how the threatening situation developed: did the threat occur suddenly or did it come about gradually?;
> - how the characters felt at different stages;
> - dramatic re-creation of moments of fear;
> - significant details of the place, people and events in the situation;
> - how the situation was resolved – if at all.

OR

b

> **Write an article for a class magazine giving your point of view about a current issue.**

You could write about ONE of the following:
- teenagers and drugs;
- animal rights;
- music;
- fashion;
- poverty;
- children's rights;

or choose a topic of your own.

> ### Examiner's tip
> Make sure you plan and structure your article, backing your opinions with evidence and examples. Consider how you can best persuade your audience to understand your point of view.

Paper 2
Shakespeare

PAPER 2
LEVELS 4–7

Instructions to student

- This test is 1 hour 15 minutes long.

- Paper 2 is based on the three Shakespeare extracts on pages 5–12 in the English booklet.

- You should do the task for **one** of the following plays:
  Henry V
  Macbeth
  Twelfth Night

- Write your answer on separate paper.

- Your work will be assessed for your knowledge and understanding of the play and the way you express your ideas. Your spelling and handwriting will also be assessed.

- You will gain extra credit if you:
  – use details and short quotations from the scene to support your ideas;
  – comment on the language of the characters;
  – refer to other parts of the play when they fit in with your answer;
  – write about it as drama (part of a play written and performed for an audience).

- Check your work carefully.

Paper 2

Choose **ONE** task.

EITHER

Henry V
Act 4 Scene 1

(From the appearance of Pistol to the end of Henry's soliloquy.)

1. It is the night before the Battle of Agincourt. The scene is set in the English Camp at Agincourt. Shakespeare uses this scene to debate a king's responsibility for war. Henry has borrowed Erpingham's cloak and, using this as a disguise, talks to some of the ordinary soldiers, including Pistol.

> **Imagine that you are Pistol in this scene.
> What are your thoughts?**

Before you begin to write you should think about:

- what the ordinary soldiers say to each other and to Henry;
- what Henry was like when he was Prince Hal;
- what the audience already know about Pistol, Bardolph, Fluellen and Falstaff;
- what Henry himself says about the duties and responsibilities of a king.

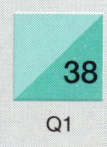

OR

Macbeth
Act 1 Scene 7

2 This is the scene in which Macbeth struggles with his conscience, loses the struggle and so chooses his fate. Macbeth's fate will be a tragic one because his ambition allows Lady Macbeth to influence him against his own, better, judgement. At this point in the play Shakespeare presents Macbeth as a hero with a choice; a hero loved and trusted by Duncan.

> **Show how Macbeth struggles with his conscience, and the important part played by Lady Macbeth in this scene.**

Before you begin to write you should consider:

- what has happened in the play before this scene;
- Macbeth's arguments against killing Duncan (lines 3–28);
- what Lady Macbeth says when Macbeth tells her he has changed his mind (lines 35–60);
- the way the murder will be carried out (lines 60–70).

OR

Twelfth Night
Act 1 Scene 5, Lines 136–253

3 Viola (disguised as Cesario) enters. She has come to woo Olivia on behalf of Orsino.

> **What more does the audience learn about Olivia and Viola in this part of the play?**

Before you begin to write you should think about:

- the situation;
- what more we learn about the two characters;
- what is interesting and entertaining for the audience;
- the way language is used.

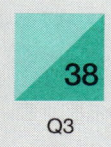

Answers

How to approach Paper 1

You will be asked to show only skills which have been a part of your Key Stage 3 studies.

SECTIONS A–B
These sections are about your ability as a reader, understanding and processing information and ideas and explaining how writers have conveyed these.

Marks available for questions 1, 2 and 3 vary. Try to divide your time accordingly. An answer worth 11 marks should take almost twice as long to construct as one with 6 marks. (This doesn't mean your answer has to be twice as long.) In a test situation this will not always work out – don't spend too much test time looking at your watch.

At the beginning of Paper One you will have 15 minutes to read the paper and make notes. You will not be allowed to write your answers until you are told to do so. Spend ten of the fifteen minutes working out:

- the CONTENT – what is each text about?
- what is the writer's PURPOSE?
- what EFFECT does each text have on you, the reader?
- how is this achieved through the use of LANGUAGE?
- who are the AUDIENCE?
- how is each text ORGANISED?

These are the things to consider whatever types of texts are used in the test paper.

> **Examiner's tip**
>
> Annotate (write on) the passages in the booklet:
> - use sub-headings;
> - underline key words and phrases;
> - divide the text into sections;
> - circle effective language;
> - make brief notes, relevant to the text and questions.

SECTION C
Notice that there are 33 marks for this question. That's a little more than the total available for Sections A–B. Try to organise your time accordingly.

The examiner will be focused on the *quality* of your written response rather than the quantity. Treat this test as an opportunity to show what your teachers have helped you to learn about being a better writer. The test only offers you limited scope to do this – but this is true for everyone else who takes it.

At its best, your answer will confirm decisions your teacher has made about the developing quality of your work during Key Stage 3.

The following pages take you through how to approach each question in turn. Read this section before you attempt your own answers. When you have completed the test, turn to the Assessment Criteria for each question to discover how to mark your test. You will also find examples of how these criteria have been specifically applied to some sample answers. Read these sample answers and then mark your own test using the same criteria.

Paper 1 Answers

How to approach Section A   Question 1

REMINDER OF THE TASK
The first 61 lines describe what Andres sees and does.

How does the writer show the reader what is happening and how Andres is involved?

In your answer you should comment on:

- the way the writer uses physical details;
- how Andres' reactions and feelings change;
- what Andres thinks and feels.

Refer to words and phrases from the passage to support your ideas.

> **Examiner's tip**
>
> Notice details that help you to imagine what it is like for Andres to be in that situation. Refer to these details in your answer. Your answer should show the development in his reactions to the changing situation.

KEY POINTS
Your answer could refer to some of the following key points:

What is happening to the prisoners	What Andres does	What Andres thinks and feels
they are beaten if they hesitate;	stays clear of the crowd;	desperate to get through the crowd;
Andres' friend jumps from the truck;	watches the truck arrive;	fears the American has a gun;
the last prisoners are driven from the truck;	sees his friend;	feels a thrill of hope about the presence of a pressman;
one who is too slow is beaten.	follows 'the American';	forgets his own danger out of concern for his friend.
	gets the crowd to part;	
	accepts his camera.	

10

Paper 1 Answers

How to approach Section A — Question 2

REMINDER OF THE TASK
Read the rest of the passage from line 62 to the end.

How effectively do you think this section builds up a picture of increasing danger yet gives hope of Andres doing something about the violence?

In your answer you should comment on:

- how the writer uses details of the soldier's violence;
- the American photographer, his role and importance;
- the behaviour of the soldiers;
- Andres' reactions.

You should support your ideas with words and phrases from the passage.

Examiner's tip

Show that you understand:
- what the extract is about (CONTENT, PURPOSE);
- what techniques the writer uses to build up a sense of danger (LANGUAGE, EFFECT);
- what techniques the writer uses to suggest a sense of hope (ORGANISATION, LANGUAGE).

Use examples from the text in your answer and try to explain their effect on the reader.

Do not just list the events. Try to show *how* the feeling of danger increases and *how* a sense of hope develops. Link your answer to the lead question.

KEY POINTS
Your answer could refer to some of the following key points:

The American photographer	The behaviour of the soldiers	Andres' reactions
he cannot be saved by the crowd;	their beating of the American photographer;	initially a helpless onlooker;
he is a victim of violence (answers may refer to how this is conveyed);	their search for the camera;	overcome by the strength of the Junta;
the soldiers are searching for his camera;	their flinging of the American photographer out of the stadium.	realisation that the film is important proof of the military's brutality;
he is an American citizen (answers may develop the significance of this).		witness of brutality to an American citizen;
		new-found sense of purpose.

Paper 1 Answers

How to approach Section B   Question 3

REMINDER OF THE TASK
The web pages are designed to interest and involve people in Oxfam's Education Now! campaign. How do the pages do this?

In your answer you should comment on:
- the information given;
- the language used;
- the way layout and images are used.

Examiner's tip

Quickly get to grips with the CONTENT of the pages; what are they about? Work out who the AUDIENCE might be and how the designer/writer of the web pages has achieved their PURPOSE (the purpose is stated in the question). ORGANISATION and LANGUAGE (and in this case graphics) are the means used to achieve several EFFECTS. What are these intended effects?

KEY POINTS
Your answer could refer to some of the following key points:

Content and layout
- photographs of people are involved;
- bold type to highlight direct speech, introduce Regina and Mwange and emphasise key points and features;
- clarity of the layout.

Language
- different voices (narrative, as well as direct speech from real people);
- informal language in direct speech;
- short paragraphs;
- clear, informative statements;
- imperatives (e.g. 'Take action now!');
- many paragraphs connected with an idea from a previous one to form a narrative.

How the reader can be involved
- 'Take action now';
- move to other stories or more detail;
- take up Oxfam's free Internet access offer.

Paper 1 Answers

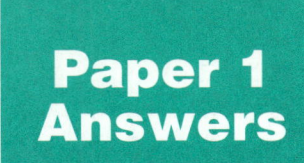

How to approach Section C — Question 4a

REMINDER OF THE TASK

Write about a threatening situation. You could write about a real or an imaginary event. Try to build up a feeling of tension or suspense.

In your answer you could include:

- how the threatening situation developed: did the threat occur suddenly or did it develop gradually?;
- how the characters felt at different stages;
- dramatic re-creation of moments of fear;
- significant details of the place, people and events in the situation;
- how the situation was resolved – if at all.

> ### Examiner's tip
>
> In your answer you are being asked to:
> - show that you can present content so as to engage and sustain the interest of the reader;
> - structure sequences of events and ideas in ways that make meaning clear to a reader;
> - sustain a chosen style;
> - write accurately.
>
> A well-structured piece of writing will be more successful than a long rambling one.
> Try to remember the following when structuring your writing:
> - aim for a strong beginning and a clear, shaped ending;
> - paragraph your writing to indicate the main elements and turning points;
> - vary your sentence structure;
> - use a wide range of vocabulary;
> - include appropriate detail to bring the writing alive;
> - check your writing for spelling and punctuation.

KEY POINTS

Your answer will be improved if you:

Plan your writing

- choose a subject or setting with which you have some familiarity;
- centre your writing around a simple plot which shows how the situation developed;
- begin with an interesting opening;
- vary the pace and feature a small number of characters and a single setting;
- explore the changing emotions and feelings of the main characters;
- use interesting and varied language, including some dialogue, to convey significant details of places, people and events;
- try to end with some sort of self-knowledge or high/low points.

Paper 1 Answers

How to approach Section C   Question 4b

REMINDER OF THE TASK
Write an article for your class magazine giving your point of view about a current issue.

You could write about:

- teenagers and drugs;
- animal rights;
- music;
- or choose a topic of your own.
- fashion;
- poverty;
- children's rights;

Examiner's tip

Write about a subject you know something about. Quickly brainstorm your ideas to plan your answer. Remember you have 15 minutes to read the paper and make notes. Your brainstorm and plan for Question 4 could be done during part of this time.

KEY POINTS
In your answer, you should try to:

- develop reasons and examples to support your opinions;
- write in a way that gets and keeps the reader's attention;
- use different ways of persuading your reader to agree with you;
- start with a clear opinion and end with a clear opinion;
- use paragraphs to structure your writing;
- use a variety of types of sentences.

Examiner's tip

Whichever part you choose to answer for Question 4 on this test, you may find it helpful to tackle the alternative on another occasion, to give yourself a chance to improve your ability to answer a different type of writing question. Remember, you complete this section at the end of Paper 1. You may become pressurised for time. However, you will be rewarded for what you have written even if your handwriting at the end is not as neat as it could be.

Paper 1 Answers

How to mark Paper 1

How to mark Section A — Question 1

The criteria that follow should be used to assess your answer for Question 1.

ASSESSMENT CRITERIA	Yes	No	Marks
Well-selected relevant references to the details of the extract.	☐	☐	(1)
Explanation of how language is used.	☐	☐	(1)
Insight into the way the reader is shown Andres' point of view.	☐	☐	(1)
Grasp of more complex ideas, e.g. importance of photographic evidence.	☐	☐	(1)
Details of the relationship between Andres' reaction and his state of mind.	☐	☐	(1)
Comments on the behaviour of the people being made relevant to Andres' reactions.	☐	☐	(1)
Total			(6)

Award yourself 1 mark for every assessment criteria to which you were able to respond 'yes'. A sample answer has been marked for you on page 16.

Marks	Level
0–2	Level 4
3	Level 5
4	Level 6
5	Level 7
6	Level 7+

Paper 1 Answers

Ben's answer to Question 1

Consider this answer to Question 1, written by Ben, a Year 9 student. What level would you give it? Refer back to the assessment criteria on page 15.

The situation in which Andres finds himself is clearly so confused and chaotic that his feelings seem to change in each paragraph. This confusion is shown in the urgency of the language. The prisoners are being treated brutally. The brutality and its effects are described, for example: 'hastened on their way with rifle butts', '"Move, scum!"', 'A stream of blood had congealed down one side of his face', 'One was not fast enough to please his guards. He was hurt, hobbling, gripping his side in pain', 'A rifle butt swung against the stumbling prisoner'.

'Andres stayed clear of the crowd … Andres broke forward.' Andres tries to reach his friend and follows the tall American. He feels hopeful, for this is a journalist. He attracts the soldiers, giving the American a chance to photograph their brutality. He hides the American's camera for him.

When he sees Braulio, looking battered but unbowed, it makes him forget the danger he himself is in and push forward to help his friend. Similarly, his response to the arrival of Don Chailey begins with a fear that the American is armed and will attract danger, then changes to a near jubilation that an outsider is coming to aid the resistance and record the brutalities that are going on.

Since the passage is written largely from Andres' perspective it allows us to see the way in which his feelings are in chaos mirroring the chaos around him, and suggests the way in which danger and exhaustion heighten his emotions.

Assessment of Ben's answer

Compare Ben's answer to the key points on page 10 and the assessment criteria on page 15.

- He presents his ideas very confidently.
- He sets about answering the tasks quickly.
- He makes many relevant references to the extract.
- He is able to keep control of long sentences containing a number of ideas – look at the last sentence, for example.
- Despite the pressures of time, in his actual test answer Ben's handwriting was clear and his spelling and punctuation were mainly correct.
- His ideas are clearly connected using words such as 'this', 'then', 'when', 'similarly', 'since'.
- He doesn't simply retell the events of the passages.
- He explains how language is used.

Ben's piece merits Level 7+. He refers closely to the text, is sensitive to its inferences, has a clear grasp of complex ideas and links different parts of his answer to each other. Furthermore, he is aware of the way in which language is used to create effect.

Paper 1 Answers

How to mark Section A — Question 2

Check your answer, identifying which of these features are present.

A sample answer on page 18 has been marked for you.

ASSESSMENT CRITERIA	Yes	No	Marks
Details of how the brutality of the soldiers is shown.	☐	☐	(1)
Language features such as similes, verbs.	☐	☐	(2)
Contrast between powerful soldiers/defenceless cameraman.	☐	☐	(2)
The way we are shown the situation from Andres' viewpoint.	☐	☐	(1)
Andres' realisation that there is something that can be done.	☐	☐	(2)
Andres' changing emotions and how they are conveyed.	☐	☐	(2)
An overview, offering an opinion of how successful the author has been.	☐	☐	(1)
Total			(11)

Marks	Level
0–4	Level 4
5–6	Level 5
7–8	Level 6
9–10	Level 7
11	Level 7+

Paper 1 Answers

Ben's answer to Question 2

Now consider this answer to Question 2, also written by Ben. What level would you give it? Refer to the assessment criteria on page 17.

The danger is shown in a vivid description of the soldiers attacking the American. His head is unprotected, in contrast to the soldiers, who wear helmets. The boots are iron clad against the vulnerable body, head and hands. Individuals in the crowd are endangered as the soldiers use violence in their efforts to find the camera. The author makes time stand still for Andres. He uses a vivid simile, 'trembled as if touched by an electrified fence', to show Andres' state of shock. He juxtaposes the vulnerability of an individual with the strong brutality of an armed dictatorship.

The American photographer is being attacked by the soldiers because they know how damaging the pictures are. They are searching for the camera and do not know that Andres has it. This is Andres' chance to do something that will affect the future behaviour of the soldiers. He knew that what was in the camera was 'just as valuable as bullets'. The pictures were proof of the soldiers' brutality towards an American citizen. Suddenly Andres has a chance of stopping any more of this violence in the future. He is not just another face in the crowd: 'All at once he had a purpose, a direction, a next step.'

Assessment of Ben's answer

Ben's answer to Question 2, although briefer, concentrates on the key words of the question – 'danger' and 'stopping this violence'. Check his answer against the key points on page 11 and the assessment criteria on page 17.

Ben refers economically to a number of important points. He does not get drawn into long repetition of the text, choosing instead to give an overview of the important points.

- He recognises the significance of the American photographer and his camera.
- He shows how Andres' reactions change.
- He recognises the relationship between the power of the soldiers and the confusion amongst the people.

Ben's answer to Question 2 is as good as his answer to Question 1. He shows an understanding of the significance of the passage and the techniques used by the writer, such as description, juxtaposition and simile. There is appreciation of the writing as a whole and relevant reference to the text. Although this answer is not as long as his answer to Question 1, it is of a very high quality – a Level 7+ is appropriate.

Paper 1 Answers

How to mark Section B — Question 3

Use the following assessment criteria to mark your answer to Question 3.
A sample answer on page 20 has been marked for you.

ASSESSMENT CRITERIA	Yes	No	Marks
Details of layout, presentational devices, headlines, photographs, bold print.	☐	☐	(2)
Understanding of the structure of the text.	☐	☐	(2)
Language features such as imperatives and direct speech explained.	☐	☐	(2)
Recognition of what the pages are trying to do and their effect on the reader.	☐	☐	(2)
The realities of life for Regina, Mwange and family, and other evidence.	☐	☐	(2)
How the reader can be involved through the Internet.	☐	☐	(1)
Total			(11)

Marks	Level
0–4	Level 4
5–6	Level 5
7–8	Level 6
9–10	Level 7
11	Level 7+

Paper 1 Answers

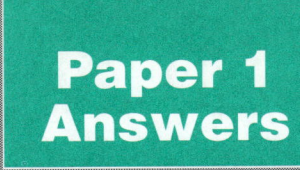

Ben's answer to Question 3

Read Ben's answer to Question 3 and then refer back to the assessment criteria on page 19.

The first page appears quite dull. There is little to interest a young reader, just factual paragraphs giving information. I imagine this web site is aimed at teachers not young people. It becomes more interesting when it gives evidence about shortages of books, desks, toilets and classrooms, and the two million children not in school. The reader will be able to compare this with schools in their own country and see the problems of people in Tanzania. The page ends with a way of helping. It doesn't explain what debt relief is.

The headline may have made the reader consider the meaning of 'Free'. Bold type shows key ideas.

The next page is much more interesting with two real life case studies, photographs and direct speech from people in Tanzania. Regina's words seem direct, and informative, and we learn about Mwange's poverty and how it affects her daughters. Her words are quoted but they do not sound like real speech. She says "Education helps me to take care of my children and keep them healthy". The text will make the reader think about education differently.

The web site tries to make you interact at the end. An imperative command, 'Take action now!' is given and you can click onto other sites and learn more.

Assessment of Ben's answer

In this excellent answer, Ben recognises the use of bold type and headlines and how photographs add to our interest: 'The first paragraph appears quite dull …', 'The next page is more interesting …'.

He shows recognition of the structure of the text: 'It becomes more interesting when it gives evidence …', 'The page ends …', '… tries to make you interact …'.

He mentions language features and understands their effect: 'Regina's words seem direct and informative…', 'An imperative command …'.

The purposes of the text are referred to: 'aimed at teachers', '… see the problems of people in Tanzania'.

Ben grasps the effect on the reader: '… will make the reader think … differently.'.

He knows how evidence is used: '… the shortage of books, desks, toilets and classrooms', '… we learn about Mwange's poverty.'

He also shows how particular features of a web site can involve the reader: 'We can help through the Internet.'

Examiner's tip

Remember, Questions 1–3 assess reading, not writing. Even if your answer is not expressed perfectly, you will gain marks if you show evidence of your understanding.

Checking against the criteria, Ben's is a Level 7+ answer.

Paper 1 Answers

How to mark Section C   Question 4a   Marking the story

Use the following assessment criteria to mark your answer.
A sample answer has been marked for you on page 24.

ASSESSMENT CRITERIA	Yes	No	Marks
Accurate spelling and fluent, clear handwriting.	☐	☐	(3)
Paragraphs used.	☐	☐	(3)
Punctuation used to clarify meaning.	☐	☐	(3)
Different sorts of sentences used to create effects.	☐	☐	(3)
Interesting opening/ending.	☐	☐	(3)
Sense of place.	☐	☐	(3)
Sense of character(s).	☐	☐	(3)
Descriptive details.	☐	☐	(3)
Range of vocabulary.	☐	☐	(3)
Insights into motivation/behaviour.	☐	☐	(3)
Is the world of the story believable?	☐	☐	(3)
Total			(33)

Look for evidence of each of these criteria in your answer.
For each one give your marks as suggested below:

No evidence? No mark.
A little evidence? 1 mark.
Some evidence? 2 marks.
Good evidence? 3 marks.

Marks	Level
0–6	Level 3
7–12	Level 4
13–18	Level 5
19–24	Level 6
25–30	Level 7
31–33	Level 7+

Paper 1 Answers

How to mark Section C   Question 4b   Marking 'Your Point of View' article.

Use the following assessment criteria to mark your answer.
A sample answer has been marked for you on page 27.

ASSESSMENT CRITERIA	Yes	No	Marks
Accurate spelling and fluent, clear handwriting.	☐	☐	(3)
Paragraphs used.	☐	☐	(3)
Punctuation used to clarify meaning.	☐	☐	(3)
Different sorts of sentences used to create effects.	☐	☐	(3)
Interesting opening.	☐	☐	(3)
Opinions clearly expressed.	☐	☐	(3)
Clear sense of how subject affects the writer's life.	☐	☐	(3)
Range of vocabulary.	☐	☐	(3)
Clear sense of the writer's point of view.	☐	☐	(3)
Gets and keeps the reader's interest.	☐	☐	(3)
A strong, clear ending.	☐	☐	(3)
		Total	(33)

Look for evidence of each of these criteria in your answer.
For each one give your marks as suggested below:

No evidence? No mark.
A little evidence? 1 mark.
Some evidence? 2 marks.
Good evidence? 3 marks.

Marks	Level
0–6	Level 3
7–12	Level 4
13–18	Level 5
19–24	Level 6
25–30	Level 7
31–33	Level 7+

Paper 1 Answers

Carrie's answer to Question 4a

Read Carrie's answer to Question 4a. What level do you think it would be? Refer to the assessment criteria on page 22.

We'd been living in the valley for about 8 years before it happened. The old barn had been completely rebuilt by my parents, using local materials and craftsmen. As a family we had been happy to leave the bustle of Birmingham and make a new life in the rural west of Wales. Mum's job as a translator could be easily done from home and Dad was happy with our fields and sheep, and restoring old furniture.

Everything was fine. The locals were friendly and it had been fun to learn Welsh in school.

Yes, everything was fine until that spring morning. The tides were unusually high, the rainfall was unending.

It came on the news but we already knew. This would be the last night that anyone in our village would be able to stay in their own homes. The constant torrents of heavy rain had caused the river to rise ever higher, the danger ever closer.

It was at a point that was maybe eight hours before it broke through the barriers, but the way it was rising, it seemed like it wouldn't last four, let alone eight. Mum decided that we wouldn't risk staying.

All our most precious belongings had been stored upstairs. We prayed that those would be safe – we knew no one local would loot them, and hoped no strangers would be around. It seemed unlikely, given the weather!

Dad had the Land Rover running as we crammed ourselves, the two dogs, sleeping bags and spare clothing into the back. The sheep and early lambs had been taken to temporary barns further up the valley sides. Dad was torn between driving us to safety and staying with them.

Safety! We still had to travel along the road by the foaming torrents that formed the once placid Dovey river. Visibility was down to the minimum, the faster the wipers moved the more the rain seemed to block our view of what might lay ahead.

Our progress seemed painfully slow – he kept to the crest of where he thought the road may be, along the valley towards the tiny church at the top of the hill.

Dad knew he must keep the motor running. Fortunately this ex-Army Land Rover had a vertical exhaust, but it was still touch and go. None of the children spoke – leaving him to drive and Mum to 'navigate'.

'We should have bought a boat,' he muttered.

Soon the worst was over. The church, like a beacon, called us ever closer to its welcome light. It had been specially opened up for all who lived on the river banks, a refuge in case the barriers should burst and flood our homes.

By morning the church was crammed full. The river had flooded most of the village and we were marooned on this hilltop. I thought of our barn and how eight years of work would now be ruined, the belongings we hadn't been able to move floating around.

Paper 1 Answers

Ours was a strong community. People shared any food they had brought, calor gas heaters added to the radiators of the church.
We had faced danger and survived!

Assessment of Carrie's answer

Carrie's answer to Question 4a achieves a Level 7+ for the following reasons:

- she shows a confident, assured style and the opening is interesting;
- the drama is well developed, building up from the calm, stable setting "until that spring morning";
- character is not only well depicted at the start, but is developed throughout the piece;
- there is a strong sense of the nature of community and of the differences between life in Birmingham and life in the Welsh countryside;
- the writing is well paragraphed - on the whole paragraphs are short, dialogue is correctly presented and the paragraphs keep the story moving;
- punctuation is accurate and clarifies meaning;
- complex, compound and simple sentences are used;
- spelling is accurate;
- there is a good variety of vocabulary ranging from the formal ("visibility was down to a minimum") to the informal ("the church was crammed full") in a natural, seemingly effortless way;
- there is variation in narrative voice: "Yes, everything was fine …", "We prayed that those would be safe …", "Dad knew he must keep the motor running", "By morning the church was crammed full", and "I thought of our barn …";
- the world of the story is believable;
- there is an insight into motivation and behaviour.

Paper 1 Answers

John's answer to Question 4b

This answer to 4b was written by John, a Year 9 student. It is reproduced here in his actual handwriting. What level do you think it could attain? Refer to the assessment criteria on page 22.

> "Following fashion is a waste of money"
>
> Following fashion is a waste of money, things these days that are involved with fashion are really a waste of money, they are so expensive. Say an outfit is in and you can only afford to buy the top but if you just wear the top then you look stupid because you are only wearing half the outfit because you can't afford the other half! If we all follow fashion we will all look the same like a can of baked beans that all look alike. The point of having clothes is to be unique, if you want to attract attention following the fashion is not the way to go about it. If you see a man with long green hair a fake knife head band looking like he has been stabbed through the head wearing a silver/metallic spacesuit and you also see a person wearing the latest GUCCI shoes who would attract YOUR attention you would look at the punk man wouldn't you?
>
> All attention seekers can't follow fashion if they want to be noticed. Normal teenagers can't always walk around in all the latest 'Cat Walk' fashion simply because the prices are unbelievably high. but I'm sure every girl out there does own a fashion item simply because of peer pressure, particulary the unpopular people they don't want to feel

'out of it' they don't want to feel odd and not in with everyone else so they probably have the most designer labels and fashion items, they don't want to be noticed, because they feel insecure about themselves.

My idea is for everyone to show off their personality through their clothes but if everybody is in dull, dark black clothes how can their personality radiate through?

If someone was loud they should wear a loud T-shirt or a bright coloured top, if someone was funny they should wear a comical T-shirt but if someone was shy and insecure then I can understand why someone may want to pay these high prices to feel with the crowd.

For me, I used to care about what I wore, meaning designer labels but now I wear what is in my price range, looks smart and is comfortable I don't care what other people might say as long as I'm happy inside no one can change my mind and I feel comfortable. It is as the saying

Paper 1 Answers

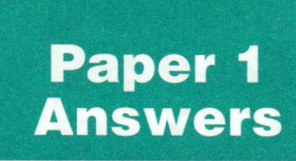

Assessment of John's answer

This is an interesting article. John's ideas are clearly expressed and the reader's interest is maintained. We learn about his opinions, the effects of fashion on himself and others and the ways he copes with it. His choice of a subject which he has already thought about and has opinions about is a strength.

Examiner's tip

You cannot write well about an issue you don't care about and have no opinions about.

John's answer to Question 4b achieves a Level 7+ for the following reasons:

- he has paragraphed his work quite successfully to structure his argument;
- he begins by stating his basic opinion and paragraph two then backs this up with more detailed examples and attempts at humour;
- paragraph three is about other teenagers and how their lives are affected by fashion;
- the next, quite short paragraph, links self-expression with fashion, and is an attempt to persuade the reader to his point of view;
- this idea is developed in paragraph five and he uses the last paragraph to conclude his argument. The test requires you to show that you can structure whole texts, with a good opening, developed ideas and an effective ending;
- John has used a range of techniques to put across his views. There are rhetorical questions, e.g. "You would look at the punk man wouldn't you?";
- he puts his views forward clearly and with coherence, so that they hold together;
- he uses quotation marks to show when he's using non-standard English, e.g. "Out of it";
- he avoids simple sentences; there are usually a number of ideas in each sentence;
- this is a good answer but a good answer is unlikely to be perfect in every respect. Would it be better if there had been some simple sentences? Would the writing have been clearer and made more impact? For example: "The point of having clothes is to be unique, if you want to attract attention following the fashion is not the way to go about it.", could have been more effectively written as two separate sentences;
- John's handwriting is generally legible. Remember he's writing under exam conditions;
- his spelling is very secure.

Paper 2 Answers

How to approach Paper 2

As with Paper 1, it is important to think through your answer to Paper 2, the Shakespeare paper. You only have to answer one question. Choose a question for the play you have studied: *Henry V* or *Macbeth* or *Twelfth Night*.

During your work at school on the set play, you will have had many opportunities to demonstrate your writing and reading skills. Many of these involved the drafting and redrafting of your answers. You will also have read the whole play and had a chance to develop a sense of the plot; establish for yourself the main characters and their characteristics; and work out how the chosen lines relate to the whole play. Think about the main themes and other aspects, like the dramatic tension and the language used. You may even have acted parts out at school or seen a production.

For this test, you will have to pace your writing so that you answer as well as you can within the time limit. You are asked to complete one task in relation to one extract. The Shakespeare paper is designed to assess your ability to understand and respond to:

- Shakespeare's presentation of ideas;
- the motivation and behaviour of characters;
- the development of the plot;
- the language of the scene you choose;
- the overall impact of the scene you choose;
- the presentation of the scenes on stage.

It is also designed to assess your ability to:

- write in a style appropriate to the task;
- organise writing clearly, using paragraphs where appropriate;
- use grammatical structures and vocabulary suitable for the clear expression of meaning;
- use a variety of sentence structures;
- use accurate punctuation and spelling;
- write clearly and legibly.

Examiner's tip

The best way to start your answer is to re-read the extract to remind yourself of its qualities and of its place in the play. You should then look again at the task and note the key words in it: what exactly is it asking you to look at and comment on? The next stage is to make notes, then to organise the main elements of your answer. You can make notes on the text, by underlining or circling important passages and lines. Such preparation will help you write a better answer.

The following pages take you through how to approach each question in turn. Read the approach for the task you have selected first. This section will give you pointers about what you should include in your answer. Then turn to the relevant assessment criteria for your question. You will find an example of how these criteria have been specifically applied to a model answer. Read the model answer and commentary, and then mark your test using the same criteria.

Paper 2 Answers

How to approach Task 1 — Henry V

REMINDER OF THE TASK
It is the night before the Battle of Agincourt. The scene is set in the English Camp at Agincourt. Shakespeare uses this scene to debate a King's responsibility for war. Henry has borrowed Erpingham's cloak and, using this a disguise, talks to some of the ordinary soldiers including Pistol.

Imagine that you are Pistol in this scene. What are your thoughts?

Before you begin to write you should think about:

- what the ordinary soldiers say to each other and to Henry;
- what Henry was like when he was Prince Hal;
- what the audience already know about Pistol, Bardolph, Fluellen and Falstaff;
- what Henry himself says about the duties and responsibilities of a king.

Examiner's tip
When Henry was Prince Hal he used to absent himself from the Court to go drinking with 'the riff-raff' of the taverns. Pistol was once one of his drinking companions, as was Falstaff and Bardolph. Bardolph's hanging in Act 3 Scene 6 will have had an impact on Pistol and will have altered his opinion of the king. Prince Hal always said that he would change once he became king but Pistol was slow to believe him. However, this scene confirms that Henry has changed and Shakespeare uses this to show the audience what the duties and responsibilities of a king are during war. You have to show the opinions of Pistol, the opinions of the ordinary soldiers and the opinions of Henry all through Pistol's point of view. A good way to do this would be to imagine that Pistol is not taken in by Henry's disguise and so knows that it is the king who is speaking.

KEY POINTS
Your answer could include some of the following key points:

- that you imagine Pistol recognises the king even though Henry is in disguise;
- Pistol eavesdropping on Henry's conversations with ordinary soldiers;
- some of the duties and responsibilities of a king in time of war;
- that Pistol is a coward;
- that there are limits to the things that a king can be held responsible for.

Paper 2 Answers

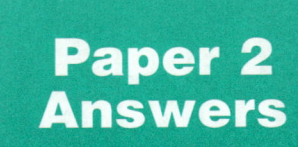

How to approach Task 2 — Macbeth

REMINDER OF THE TASK
This is the scene in which Macbeth struggles with his conscience, loses the struggle and so chooses his fate. Macbeth's fate will be a tragic one because his ambition allows Lady Macbeth to influence him against his own, better, judgement. At this point in the play Shakespeare presents Macbeth as a hero with a choice; a hero loved and trusted by Duncan.

Show how Macbeth struggles with his conscience, and the important part played by Lady Macbeth in this scene.

Before you begin to write you should consider:

- what has happened in the play before this scene;
- Macbeth's arguments against killing Duncan (lines 3–28);
- what Lady Macbeth says when Macbeth tells her he has changed his mind (lines 35–60);
- the way the murder will be carried out (lines 60–70).

Examiner's tip

The stage is busy with Macbeth's butler and servants preparing a hospitable and celebratory feast for Duncan, King of Scotland. This is Macbeth's castle. Macbeth enters by himself. He takes no notice of the work going on in the Great Hall because he is pre-occupied with thoughts of the consequences of murdering the King. He is struggling with his conscience. He decides not to kill Duncan. Lady Macbeth appears and he tells his wife that he has changed his mind. She is furious. She accuses him of being a coward and of not being a proper man. She outlines a plan that shows how easy it would be to kill Duncan and blame other people for the murder. Macbeth changes his mind again. His ambition and his wife's ambition will now lead them both along a bloody and a tragic path.

KEY POINTS
Your answer could include some of the following points:

- the idea that Macbeth chose his fate and his tragedy;
- an explanation of why Lady Macbeth was so angry with her husband;
- the part played by the Witches before this scene;
- the association of pity and fear with kindness and decent behaviour.

Paper 2 Answers

How to approach Task 3 — Twelfth Night

REMINDER OF THE TASK
Viola (disguised as Cesario) enters. She has come to woo Olivia on behalf of Orsino.

What more does the audience learn about Olivia and Viola in this part of the play?

Before you begin to write you should think about:

- the situation;
- what more we learn about the two characters;
- what is interesting and entertaining for the audience;
- the way language is used.

Examiner's tip

We already know quite a lot about Olivia at this stage in the play. She is the object of, but does not return, Duke Orsino's romantic fantasies. Like him she has a false view of self. She is exaggeratedly mourning her father and brother's deaths and rejecting pleasure and love. This is not her true nature and this is hinted at earlier in this scene when being teased by her fool, and in her dismissal of Malvolio as being 'sick of self-love'. The shipwrecked Viola (who does not yet know if her twin brother lives) is already deceiving Orsino in her disguise as a man. In this role she has found herself falling in love with him. In Shakespeare's time, Viola would have been played by a boy – adding to the audience's amusement, confusion and disquiet. She is the play's 'heroine', freeing Olivia and Orsino from their warped views of themselves. In this scene we see Viola (as Cesario) wooing Olivia on Orsino's behalf. The complications of disguise and deception are increased as Olivia falls in love with 'him'.

KEY POINTS
Your answer could refer to some of the following points:

- what we already know about each character;
- what Olivia and Viola have in common;
- how the themes of the play (e.g. disguise, illusion) are developed;
- how the behaviour of each woman changes;
- the variety of language used;
- the effect of disguise and illusion on the audience.

Paper 2 Answers

How to mark Paper 2

This paper will try to assess both your reading ability and your writing ability. Your reading will be assessed in terms of your understanding and response to the text. To mark your understanding and response, find the specific assessment criteria for the question you answered.

How to mark Task 1   Henry V

First, mark your understanding and response by considering the questions below:

SHAKESPEARE ASSESSMENT CRITERIA: UNDERSTANDING AND RESPONSE	Yes	No
Is Agincourt mentioned?	☐	☐
Is the fact that the English army is heavily outnumbered mentioned?	☐	☐
Has anything been said about how Henry behaved as Prince Hal?	☐	☐
Has anything been said about the friendship between Bardolph, Pistol and Henry in the old days before Henry was King?	☐	☐
Has Fluellen been mentioned?	☐	☐
Has the manner and significance of Bardolph's death been explained?	☐	☐
Does the answer mention some of the views of the ordinary soldiers?	☐	☐
Does the answer try to see events from Pistol's point of view?	☐	☐
Has Pistol tried to imagine how Henry might see events now that he is king?	☐	☐
Has Henry's disguise and conversation with ordinary soldiers been mentioned?	☐	☐
Have some of the actual words spoken by the characters been used?	☐	☐

Award yourself 2 marks for every assessment question for which you were able to respond 'yes' (22 marks total). The following chart will give you an indication of the level at which you are working, in terms of your understanding and response:

Your score	Level
2–4 marks	Level 3
6–8 marks	Level 4
10–12 marks	Level 5
14–16 marks	Level 6
18–20 marks	Level 7
22 marks	Level 7+

Enter your marks for Understanding and Response on the Marking Grid on page 46. Then mark your Written Expression using the general criteria on pages 44–5. Enter your marks for Written Expression on the Marking Grid on page 46. You will find that the following sample answer has been marked using the same criteria (see page 35).

Paper 2 Answers

Luke's answer to Task 1

Consider this answer to Task 1. Refer to the assessment criteria for Understanding and Response for this scene on page 32 and to the general assessment criteria for Written Expression on pages 44–5. What level do you think it deserves? The answer is assessed on page 35.

It is night time at Agincourt. Tomorrow we are going to fight the French and we are all most likely going to be killed.

I followed the King to France in the hope of doing well and instead here I am at Agincourt. I wanted to make some money and having a King as a friend it should have been easy. So far I've made no money and after what has happened to Bardolph I dare not steal anything. Bardolph was caught stealing a small, silver pax from a French church and has been hanged for it. Fluellen wouldn't speak for Bardolph's life even although I asked him to. Prince Hal must have known that his friend was going to be hanged but he didn't do anything to save him either.

Now that he is King Henry the Fifth, Prince Hal has changed. Bardolph used to be his friend but he has been hanged as a thief. I was Hal's friend and my life is at risk. At Harfleur I was forced to get close to the fighting by that damned Welsh scoundrel, Fluellen, and now I am going to be killed or at least badly wounded by the French here at Agincourt tomorrow. Look at the danger we are in. The French army is a full three-score thousand and we English are outnumbered five to one.

What does the King think he is doing? He borrows Sir Thomas's cloak to wear as a disguise to walk around the camp and talk to us ordinary soldiers. Does he think I don't recognise the sound of his voice? What do I think of him? What I told him was that I thought him a fine fellow with 'a heart of gold' and said, 'I love the lovely bully'. The truth is I'm frightened of him.

I am dreading the approach of day. He thinks that what he is doing is honourable and his duty as a King. He knows what our situation is. He is a man and knows fear but since he has become King these feelings do not stop him. They would have done once when he used to drink with me and Falstaff. He knows that his soldiers are 'as men wrecked upon a sand, that look to be washed off the next tide', because I heard him say so to Williams.

If he really cared about our lives he would offer himself, alone, for ransom and save 'many poor men's lives', mine included. But he says he will not be ransomed. How do I know that he is not just saying this 'to make us fight cheerfully but when our throats are cut, he may be ransomed, and we ne'er the wiser'? The truth is that people like me are nothing in his plans.

People say that he's changed from what he was like before. He cannot show any fear as a leader even if he feels frightened because it might 'dishearten his army'. I thought he was one of us, happy to eat and drink, have a good time and sleep well at night. He must take responsibility for putting us into this battle. He must take responsibility for our lives and for leading us to our deaths at Agincourt. He might be the King but he cannot heal severed arms and legs. I hope the weight of that thought keeps him awake at night.

Paper 2 Answers

How do I know that this war against the French is right? What if 'all those legs, and arms, and heads, chopped off in a battle' cannot be justified by the reason for the battle? I don't want to lie dying on a battle field, swearing and crying out for a doctor. The fear and terror of it. How can I make any arrangements to sort out my affairs, to look after my wife, Nell, dying in such a way?

In any case I have not led a very good life. I have even been described as, 'a bawd, a cut-purse.' If I get killed tomorrow I'll probably go to Hell. And whose fault will that be? I think it will be the king's but I heard him say to Williams, Every subject's duty is the King's: but every subject's soul is his own'. Every soldier should be prepared for death is what he would say. That fool Williams agreed, saying, 'the ill upon his own head: the king is not to answer for it'.

I never wanted to be a soldier. I am not prepared for death. I thought I could avoid being in the kind of fight where I might get killed. If I manage to survive tomorrow's battle I'll sort out that Welsh goat, Fluellen, then go back to England and live happily with Nell.

Paper 2 Answers

Assessment of Luke's answer to Task 1

UNDERSTANDING AND RESPONSE
Luke's answer is very good.

He knows that Shakespeare uses this scene to debate some of the issues of a King's responsibility for war. He shows that he knows what some of these duties are. He also knows that he has to write about war from the point of view of Pistol.

In his answer, Luke shows that many of the views of the ordinary soldiers would also be the opinions of Pistol. However, Pistol knows more about Henry than the ordinary soldiers because as Prince Hal, Henry used to drink together with Pistol, Bardolph, Nym and Falstaff in 'The Boar's Head' before he was King of England. In trying to write from Pistol's point of view Luke has to refer to those days and to wonder at the difference between then and now. 'Now' being the night before the Battle of Agincourt. Henry is a very different character from when he was Prince Hal. This contrast is one of the dramatic devices used by Shakespeare to make the audience think about the nature of kingship and leadership.

Another problem in writing about this scene from Pistol's point of view is finding a way of giving Henry's opinions about his duties and responsibilities for the men under his command. Luke solves this difficulty quite brilliantly by imagining that the cloak Henry borrows as a disguise does not hide the King's identity from his former drinking companion, Pistol. As a result Pistol, pretending to be taken in by the disguise, is first able to flatter the king and then to eavesdrop on the conversations with other soldiers. Using this idea, Luke could even have imagined Pistol listening to Henry's private thoughts spoken aloud [soliloquy] at the end of this scene in which he considers the differences that leadership and kingship impose.

Now consider the Shakespeare Assessment Criteria on page 32. Luke's answer meets all these criteria and would therefore score 22 marks (Level 7+) for Understanding and Response.

WRITTEN EXPRESSION
The quality of expression in this answer is as high as the quality of Understanding and Response, as is demonstrated by the following positive features:

- clear use of paragraphs;
- clear expression of ideas;
- a clever use of short quotations;
- the use of the personal pronoun "I" is appropriate when writing from Pistol's point of view;
- the style of writing gives the impression that these are Pistol's thoughts;
- there is a range of accurate and helpful punctuation;
- simple and complex sentences have been used;
- the first and last paragraphs provide a clear start and a clear ending.

Using the assessment criteria on pages 44–5 to give a separate mark for Written Expression, Luke's answer should be awarded a high Level 7 (16 marks).

Paper 2 Answers

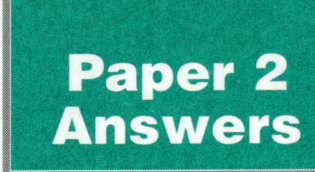

How to mark Task 2 — Macbeth

First, mark your understanding and response by considering the questions below:

SHAKESPEARE ASSESSMENT CRITERIA: UNDERSTANDING AND RESPONSE	Yes	No
Are Macbeth, Lady Macbeth and Duncan mentioned?	☐	☐
Are there relevant references to what has gone on before and after this scene?	☐	☐
Does the answer explain why Macbeth does not want to kill Duncan?	☐	☐
Does the answer explain why Macbeth changes his mind?	☐	☐
Does the answer explain what Lady Macbeth says to her husband?	☐	☐
Does the answer explain how the murder is to be carried out?	☐	☐
Have the words 'ambition' and 'tragedy' been used about the play and Macbeth?	☐	☐
Have quotations been used to support what has been said?	☐	☐
Is there some understanding of the way language has been used?	☐	☐
Has the idea of conscience been written about?	☐	☐
Has the question of what kind of qualities make a man been mentioned?	☐	☐

Award yourself 2 marks for every assessment question for which you were able to respond 'yes' (22 marks total). The following chart will give you an indication of the level at which you are working, in terms of your understanding and response:

Your score	Level
2–4 marks	Level 3
6–8 marks	Level 4
10–12 marks	Level 5
14–16 marks	Level 6
18–20 marks	Level 7
22 marks	Level 7+

Enter your marks for Understanding and Response on the Marking Grid on page 46. Then assess your Written Expression using the general criteria on pages 44–5. Enter your marks for Written Expression on the Marking Grid on page 46. The following sample answer has been marked using the same criteria (see page 39).

Paper 2 Answers

Kelly's answer to Task 2

Consider this answer to Task 2. Refer to the assessment criteria for Understanding and Response for this scene on page 36 and to the general assessment criteria for Written Expression on pages 44–5. What level do you think it deserves? The answer is assessed on page 39.

Scene 7 starts with Macbeth, alone, struggling with his conscience. He is considering the consequences for himself in this life, 'We shall have judgement here,' of the assassination, the political murder, of Duncan. If there were to be no consequences '... here, upon this bank and shoal of time...' then he would take his chances about what might happen to him in the next life. This image of the events of life and time as a flowing river recurs later in the play when once again Macbeth consider his conscience in Act 3 Scene 4 and says to Lady Macbeth:

> '... I am in blood
> Stepped in so far that should I wade no more,
> Returning were as tedious as go o'er.'

But here in Act 1 Scene 7, Macbeth has not yet started 'wading in blood'. At this point in the play he appears to be choosing not to do so as he considers the common sense and practical reasons against murdering Duncan. He would have to guard against future vengeance. He is Duncan's subject and therefore owes him loyalty. He is his relative and as Duncan is also a guest in Macbeth's house his safety and comfort is Macbeth's double responsibility. Duncan is a good and virtuous king loved by heaven. There would be widespread grief in heaven and among the people when they heard of his murder:

> '... or heaven's cherubin horsed
> Upon the sightless couriers of the air,
> Shall blow the horrid deed in every eye,
> That tears shall drown the wind.'

When Macbeth tells Lady Macbeth that he has decided 'to proceed no further in this business' she furiously asks him a whole list of insulting, rhetorical questions. She accuses him of being a drunk daydreamer and too much of a coward to really become king.

To call Macbeth a coward when he has fought bravely against Scotland's enemies raises the question of what makes a man. Macbeth protests that, 'I dare do all that may become a man' and indeed the only time in the play where he shows any fear is just after he has murdered Duncan. He should have left the daggers in the room but is too frightened to look again on what he has done. The audience is likely to think that Macbeth is right to feel fear at the sight of murder. Fear, doubt and pity seem to be a necessary part of conscience. At this point in the play Lady Macbeth does not listen to her conscience. Later her conscience will be an important cause of her madness.

Paper 2 Answers

The image of pity 'like a naked, new born babe' used by Macbeth as a reason for not murdering Duncan is used as a startlingly cruel reproach against him by Lady Macbeth:

> 'I have given suck and know
> How tender 'tis to love the babe that milks me:
> I would, while it was smiling in my face,
> Have plucked my nipple from his boneless gums
> And dashed the brains out, had I so sworn
> As you have done to this.'

She feels no pity and no fear and does not consider failure. She outlines her plan for how Duncan can be murdered. The guards will be drugged and Duncan left asleep and unguarded:

> 'What cannot you and I perform upon
> Th'unguarded Duncan?'

Afterwards these guards can be blamed for the murder. Ambition leads Macbeth to agree to the murder of Duncan and to accept Lady Macbeth's idea of the qualities that make a man:

> 'Bring forth men-children only,
> For thy undaunted mettle should compose
> Nothing but males.

The deceit and double-dealing that will now be necessary until the murder remind the audience of what Duncan said about the Thane of Cawdor:

> 'There's no art
> To find the mind's construction in the face.'

The murder of Duncan is caused by Macbeth's ambition. He has no other reason for the murder:

> 'I have no spur
> To prick the sides of my intent, but only
> Vaulting ambition'.

This is what makes the play a tragedy and causes the eventual downfall of Macbeth and Lady Macbeth.

Paper 2 Answers

Assessment of Kelly's answer to Task 2

UNDERSTANDING AND RESPONSE
Kelly's answer shows a good understanding of the importance of this scene in the play. She understands the part played by ambition in Macbeth's downfall and something of the way in which Shakespeare has written the tragedy. She knows that Macbeth's tragic flaw is ambition and that this flaw is made worse by Lady Macbeth's own ambition both for herself and her husband.

She is aware of the context of the scene in the development of the play. She gives an indication that she knows what has happened before by quoting Duncan's comment about Cawdor. This associates Macbeth with a previous traitor and connects Duncan's comment neatly to the new Thane of Cawdor who is, of course, now Macbeth himself. Kelly shows that she also knows what happens to Lady Macbeth later in the play.

Her answer is clear about Macbeth's reasons for not killing Duncan and shows how and why he is persuaded to change his mind. She is clear about the way the murder is planned by Lady Macbeth.

Her answer starts to consider the qualities of manliness through Lady Macbeth's eyes and makes very good use of appropriate quotations. She understands how language is used to create dramatic effects and recognises that certain images are important and reappear elsewhere in the play. Finally, Kelly is aware of possible effects on an audience.

Looking at the assessment criteria on page 36, it is possible to answer 'yes' to all 11 questions. Therefore, Kelly would score 22 marks (i.e. Level 7+) for Understanding and Response.

NOTE
Other possible questions about Act 1 Scene 7 might ask you to write either from the point of view of Macbeth or from the point of view of Lady Macbeth.

WRITTEN EXPRESSION
This is a well-written answer. It contains the following positive features:

- accurate and helpful punctuation;
- quite short appropriate quotations, in quotation marks and usually on separate lines;
- well handled, compound sentence structures: 'She feels no pity and no fear and does not consider failure';
- accurate spelling;
- a varied choice of words.

Looking at the assessment criteria on pages 44–5, Kelly's answer would be awarded Level 7+ (i.e. 16 marks) for Written Expression.

Paper 2 Answers

How to mark Task 3 — Twelfth Night

First, mark your understanding and response by considering the questions below:

SHAKESPEARE ASSESSMENT CRITERIA: UNDERSTANDING AND RESPONSE	Yes	No
Does the answer put the question in the context of the play so far?	☐	☐
Are relevant characters besides Olivia and Viola mentioned?	☐	☐
Are themes of deception and reality identified?	☐	☐
Is the changing character of Olivia explained with examples?	☐	☐
Is Viola's character explored with examples?	☐	☐
Does the answer explain how an audience might view this scene?	☐	☐
Is the importance of acting referred to?	☐	☐
Is there consideration of the effect of Viola on Olivia?	☐	☐
Is there consideration of Viola's interest in Olivia?	☐	☐
Is there an understanding of the different ways language is used?	☐	☐
Are the ideas supported by relevant references and quotations?	☐	☐

Award yourself 2 marks for every assessment question to which you were able to respond 'yes' (22 marks total). The following chart will give you an indication of the level at which you are working, in terms of your understanding and response:

Your score	Level
2–4 marks	Level 3
6–8 marks	Level 4
10–12 marks	Level 5
14–16 marks	Level 6
18–20 marks	Level 7
22 marks	Level 7+

Enter your marks for Understanding and Response on the Marking Grid on page 46. Then assess your Written Expression using the general criteria on pages 44–5. Enter your marks for Written Expression on the Marking Grid on page 46. The following sample answer has been marked using the same criteria.

Paper 2 Answers

Thomas' answer to Task 3

Consider this answer to Task 3. Refer to the assessment criteria for Understanding and Response for this scene on page 40 and to the general assessment criteria for Written Expression on pages 44–5. What level do you think it deserves? The answer is assessed on page 43.

Already in this scene we have seen Olivia's enjoyment of her fool's wordplay and her sharpness with the self-loving Malvolio. This helps prepare us for what is to come as our curiosity is built up for the meeting of Viola and Olivia. They have in common letters of their name and both are playing roles – one a man, one a mourner – protecting themselves from male interest.

We have heard that Olivia is young, beautiful and rich, that Duke Orsino thinks he loves her, that she rejects him and, according to her uncle, Sir Toby, will not marry anyone more wealthy, powerful, older or cleverer than herself. The audience know much about Viola; a shipwreck victim who may have lost her brother, pluckily making a new life in disguise. She too is attractive but is poor. She is more practical than Olivia.

The audience sees the play's theme of deception and identity in the veiling of Olivia before Viola's entrance. She has come to woo Olivia on behalf of Orsino, her master. Later the face will be unveiled. How 'real' is what is revealed?

'We will draw a curtain and show you the picture', but can we trust what we see? Viola's 'I am not that I play' echoes this.

Olivia is going to come out of hiding and open herself to love and all that threatens. Viola will cure her of self-indulgent, self-deceiving love. Viola begins her speech (as Cesario) in over-flattering, over-complex language: 'Most radiant, exquisite and unmatchable beauty.' Unsure of who she is talking to (because of the veil) she never completes the speech so carefully prepared (perhaps by Orsino to whom she is loyal throughout the play) and lets her true nature show.

There is a dialogue of curiosity about each other:

> *'Whence come you sir?'*
> *'Are you a comedian?'*
> *'Are you the lady of the house?'*

The audience know the answers, the characters don't.

The two go on to play word games together, references to 'sail', 'swabber' and 'hull' repeating images of the sea – the means by which Viola has arrived in Illyria.

Olivia has vowed to mourn her dead brother and avoid men for seven years, but Viola's liveliness and energy win such a positive response that Olivia lifts her veil. Olivia also reveals a high opinion of her own good looks:

> *'Is't not well done?'*

Her thoughts and feelings are not so sad as she has pretended; Viola's language and appearance are winning Olivia over. Heightened poetical language, the traditional language of love, contrasts with Olivia's prose and Viola's moving and sincere lines beginning: 'Make me a willow

Paper 2 Answers

cabin at your gate', show Olivia and the audience what love is really like. We recognise how honest she is and her good sense in expressing the sincerity of love.

Olivia and Viola are fascinated by one another, the audience are fascinated by the illusion and delusions presented in the play. Acting and people as actors, assuming roles and masking their true selves, are central to our enjoyment of the play. Olivia has moved on in this world. She has looked Viola up and down and is physically attracted as well as having enjoyed her language:

> 'Thy tongue, thy face, thy limbs, actions, and spirit
> Do give thee fivefold blazon.'

'Thou' and 'thy' were words used to show you felt close to people. Olivia realises the speed of her infatuation:

> 'Not too fast! Soft, soft!'

She associates love with sickness:

> 'Even so quickly may one catch the plague?'

Love has changed her perceptions as she thinks about the 'man' that she has just met. The audience will be developing and changing their perceptions of the characters.

> 'Me thinks I feel this youth's perfections
> With an invisible and subtle stealth
> To creep in at mine eyes.'

Viola's good looks, good humour and imaginative compliments and sincerity have released the self-repressed Olivia's capacity for love.

Paper 2 Answers

Assessment of Thomas' answer to Task 3

UNDERSTANDING AND RESPONSE

This is an excellent answer. It shows a grasp of motivation and behaviour. It is a personal view based on thorough knowledge of the play. The final 'summing up' sentence shows this: 'Viola's good looks, good humour and imaginative compliments and sincerity have released the self-repressed Olivia's capacity for love.'

His understanding of the situation is shown in Thomas' first two paragraphs. He recounts what we already know about Olivia and Viola very economically and develops ideas about these characters which are relevant to the extract studied and the question answered. He helps the reader understand the situation. He does not spend too long giving evidence to back this excellent summary. He is right not to; he has more time to answer the question.

He skilfully links his account of the scene with very important themes of the play: deception, illusion and identity. His grasp of this is supported by appropriate quotations. In writing about the characters in this part of the play, he is able to identify the effect Viola is going to have on Olivia: 'Viola will cure her of self-indulgent, self-deceiving love'.

Thomas shows how double meaning and disguise will be enjoyed by the audience: 'The audience know the answers, the characters don't.' An examiner will be impressed by his grasp of the play as a performance, e.g. 'We recognise ...', 'The audience will be developing ...'.

Throughout his response, Thomas identifies the ways language is used, e.g. 'dialogue of curiosity', 'the two go on to play word games together', 'images of the sea', 'heightened poetical language', 'thou' and 'thy'... show you felt close to people.'

He recognises double meaning, explaining, 'We will draw a curtain and show you the picture', and 'I am not the play'. He could have written more about this but time limits what can be put down in an exam. The examiner will be looking for what you do know, not what you don't,

Notice that Thomas' answer responds to the points mentioned under 'Before you begin to write you should think about' (see the question). It is not necessary to write sections addressing these. Thomas refers to them at various appropriate points in his answer.

Using the assessment criteria on page 40, find out how many questions you can answer 'yes' to. All the questions? Thomas would score 22 marks (Level 7+) for Understanding and Response.

WRITTEN EXPRESSION

The writing in this answer is accurate, mature and set out well. It gives the impression of confidence, being structured in an individual, consciously crafted style. This is shown by the following positive features:

- clearly indicated paragraphs;
- short quotations from the play, written on separate lines;
- sentences are varied and all begin with a capital letter and end with a full stop;
- quotations punctuated just as they are in the play;
- the correct use of the apostrophe of possession, for example: 'Olivia's capacity for love'.
- a wide range of punctuation used, i.e. not just commas and full stops;
- clear communication of ideas by careful use of personal pronouns, i.e. using 'he', 'she' and 'they' instead of full character names when appropriate.

Using the assessment criteria on page 44–5, Thomas' answer would be awarded Level 7+ (16 marks) for Written Expression.

Paper 2 Answers

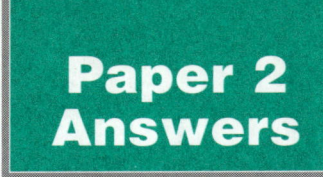

How to mark your Written Expression

Use the assessment criteria opposite. Decide which level best describes your writing following the steps below. Then award yourself the relevant number of marks, according to how well you feel your writing meets the criteria, as described below. Begin with the questions for Level 4.

If you are unable to answer 'yes' to at least two of the questions for Level 4, your written expression is probably at an earlier stage of development and you may be working at Level 3.

Award yourself 5 marks total.

If you are able to answer 'yes' to at least two of the questions for Level 4, go on to consider the questions for Level 5. If you then answer 'yes' to fewer than half the questions for Level 5, you are probably working at Level 4.

Award yourself 6 marks total.

If you are able to answer 'yes' to at least three of the Level 5 questions, you are probably working at Level 5.

Award yourself 9 marks total.

If you are able to answer 'yes' to more than half the questions for Level 5, go on to consider the questions for Level 6. If you then answer 'yes' to fewer than three of the Level 6 questions, you are probably working at Level 5.

Award yourself 9 marks total.

If you are able to answer 'yes' to at least half of the Level 6 questions, then you are probably working at Level 6.

Award yourself 12 marks total.

If you are able to answer 'yes' to at least three of the questions for Level 6, go on to consider the Level 7 questions. If you then answer 'yes' to only one or two questions for Level 7, you are probably working at Level 6.

Award yourself 12 marks total.

If you are able to answer 'yes' to at least three of the questions for Level 7, then you are probably working at Level 7.

Award yourself 15 marks total.

If you are able to answer 'yes' to most of the questions for Level 7, go on to consider the questions for Level 7+. If you then answer 'yes' to fewer than four of the Level 7+ questions, you are probably working at Level 7.

Award yourself 15 marks total.

If you are able to answer 'yes' to all of the questions for Level 7+, you are probably working at a High Level 7 or above.

Award yourself 16 marks total.

Paper 2 Answers

terribly

SHAKESPEARE ASSESSMENT CRITERIA: WRITTEN EXPRESSION	Yes	No
LEVEL 4 Are ideas generally clearly expressed, i.e. is the meaning clear to the reader? Is there some use of paragraphs? Is the punctuation to mark sentences generally accurate, with some punctuation within the sentences? Is the spelling of simple and common polysyllabic words generally accurate? Is the handwriting mostly clear and legible?	☐ ☐ ☐ ☐ ☐	☐ ☐ ☐ ☐ ☐
LEVEL 5 Are ideas clearly expressed and clearly structured, with words usually used precisely and appropriately? Are simple and complex sentences usually organised into paragraphs? Is a range of punctuation, including commas, apostrophes and quotation marks, usually used accurately? Is spelling usually accurate, including words with complex regular patterns? Is the handwriting generally clear, legible and fluent?	☐ ☐ ☐ ☐ ☐	☐ ☐ ☐ ☐ ☐
LEVEL 6 Does the writing communicate well, with ideas grouped into paragraphs with a sense of purpose? Is the vocabulary varied, with a range of appropriate language used in a range of simple and complex sentences? Is spelling accurate, though there may be errors in difficult words? Is a range of punctuation usually used correctly to clarify meaning? Is the handwriting consistently legible and fluent?	☐ ☐ ☐ ☐ ☐	☐ ☐ ☐ ☐ ☐
LEVEL 7 Is the writing confident, with assured choices of words and style appropriate for the subject? Are paragraphing and punctuation used correctly? Is the spelling perfect, except for errors caused by minor slips or through the use of specialised words? Is the handwriting consistently legible and fluent? Are grammatical features and vocabulary used accurately, appropriately and effectively?	☐ ☐ ☐ ☐ ☐	☐ ☐ ☐ ☐ ☐
LEVEL 7+ Is the writing coherent and structured in an individual, consciously crafted style? Are vocabulary and grammar used to make fine distinctions and/or to emphasise a point of view? Is the spelling and punctuation almost faultless? Is the handwriting consistently fluent and legible?	☐ ☐ ☐ ☐	☐ ☐ ☐ ☐

Grammar section
Spelling, Punctuation and Grammar

Instructions to student

- Before starting to answer questions 1–9 you should spend 10 minutes reading the **Talking in Whispers** and **Robinson Crusoe** extracts on pages 1–2 and 13–14 of the English booklet.

- Spend 1 hour on this section.

- Divide your time as follows:
  - 15 minutes on Part 1 (Sentence Level)
  - 5 minutes on Part 2 (Word Level: Spelling)
  - 8 minutes on Part 3 (Word Level: Parts of Speech)
  - 8 minutes on Part 4 (Word Level: Language Changes)
  - 16 minutes on Part 5 (Text Level)
  - 8 minutes on Part 6 (Word Level: Spelling)

- Write your answers to questions 1–4 and 8–16 on separate paper.
- Check your work carefully.

Grammar section

Start [ ]   Finish [ ]

To work on Parts 1–5 of the Grammar section you need the extracts *Talking in Whispers* and **The Life and Adventures of Robinson Crusoe** on pages 1–2 and 13–14 of the English booklet.

Part 1   Sentence Level

*Read this sentence from **Robinson Crusoe**:*

'When I came down from my appartment in the tree, I look'd about me again, and the first thing I found was the boat, which lay as the wind and the sea had toss'd her up upon the land, about two miles on my right hand.'

It is a compound sentence. This is to say that it is a series of simple sentences joined by words called connectives. Connectives are words like, 'although', 'as if', 'when', 'while', 'since', 'after'.

1   **List the four connectives used in the sentence above from *Robinson Crusoe*.**

A simple sentence is a group of words with one verb that makes sense by itself. It can stand by itself and make sense. For example, 'I came down from my appartment in the tree.', is a simple sentence.

2   **Write out the five simple sentences that have been joined by the four connectives in the sentence from *Robinson Crusoe*.**
The first one has been done for you above.

*Count the number of words in the first sentence of **Talking in Whispers** and the number of words in the first sentence, which is the entire first paragraph, of the **Robinson Crusoe** extract.*

First sentence of **Talking in Whispers**.   Number of words [   ]
First sentence of **Robinson Crusoe**.   Number of words [   ]

*Now read lines 68–70 in **Talking in Whispers**. This is probably the longest sentence in this extract, yet in the **Robinson Crusoe** extract every sentence is longer.*

Marks: Q1 = 4, Q2 = 5

Grammar section

3 Think of TWO reasons for this difference in sentence length.

[4 marks — Q3]

A phrase is a group of words (two or more) without a verb. Examples from **Talking in Whispers** *are:*

'with rifle butts'
'An American.'
'the tall one'

Read these words from **Robinson Crusoe**:

'In a word, I had nothing about me but a knife, a tobacco-pipe, and a little tobacco in a box; this was all my provision, … .'

4 How many of the words are phrases?
Why do you think so many have been used?

[6 marks — Q4]

Part 2 Word Level: Spelling

You will have learnt that language changes over time. One example of this is the way the spelling of some English words has altered. Here are some examples from **Robinson Crusoe**.

5 Provide the modern spelling of the words in bold type.
Use the box after each question for your answer.

a '**Wrapt** up in the contemplation of my deliverance'.

[1 mark — Q5a]

b 'thick bushy tree like a **firr**'.

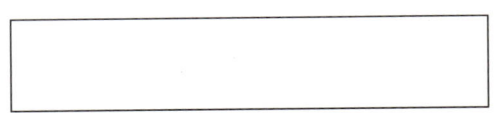

[1 mark — Q5b]

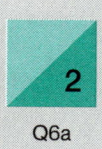

c 'consider the next day what death I should **dye**'.

[ ]

d 'by the swelling of the **tyde**'.

[ ]

e 'when I came down from my **appartment**'.

[ ]

f 'where I had **hop'd** to find something for my present subsistence'.

[ ]

Part 3 Word Level: Parts of Speech

*Look at the first paragraph of **Talking in Whispers**.*

'The prisoners who hesitated …'. 'Hesitated' is a verb. The root of this verb is 'hesitate'.

6 What part of speech is the word in bold print in each of these sentences?

a **Hesitation** always leads to delay.

Part of speech:..

b The cat crept **hesitatingly** into the pipe.

Part of speech:..

Grammar section

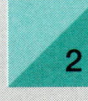

c Her **hesitant** answer showed how nervous she was.

Part of speech: ....

d **Hesitancy** in striking the ball will lead to a missed penalty.

Part of speech: ....

e He who **hesitates** is lost.

Part of speech: ....

Part 4   Word Level: Language Changes

You have just seen how spellings have changed. The meaning of words and the order in which they are used has also changed over time.

7 Here are some examples of language from *Robinson Crusoe* which we are unlikely to use nowadays. Look at the examples below and write each one as it would be written today.

a 'that there should be not one soul sav'd but myself'

....

....

b 'I cast my eyes to the stranded vessel'

....

....

c 'Night coming upon me'

....

....

Grammar section

MARKS

2 Q7d

2 Q7e

d 'expressively fatigu'd'

....

....

e 'I walk'd as far as I could upon the shore'

....

....

Part 5 Text Level

The way each of the two passages is written adds to the reader's knowledge and understanding of the situation of the two central characters. There are important differences in the way that each extract is written. The situations of Andres in the National Stadium and Robinson Crusoe on the shore have a different sense of time and a different sense of urgency. This is shown in the organisation of the sentences and paragraphs.

*In **Talking in Whispers** time is very short for Andres. Events happen quickly and each one increases Andres' involvement and danger.*

*In **Robinson Crusoe** time is not short. He may not be entirely safe but all immediate danger is past. He is at least out of the sea and on the shore. If he is to continue to survive he must notice every detail of his new surroundings. The writer also wants the reader to be able to imagine being in that situation.*

NOTE
'Contrast' in a question means that you have to point out the differences between things.

Examiner's tip
To answer Question 8 you need to find examples of how slowly the story of Robinson Crusoe develops and how quickly the story about Andres moves. Contrast the amount and kind of detail in both extracts. Contrast the length and number of paragraphs. For example, there is an astonishing example of a one-phrase paragraph in **Talking in Whispers**. (Look at the first half of **Talking in Whispers**.)

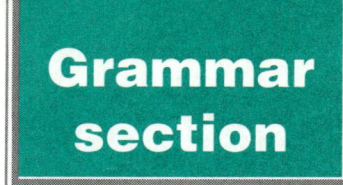

Grammar section

8 **Contrast the way the writers describe the situations of Andres in the National Stadium and Robinson Crusoe on the shore.**

[10 marks – Q8]

A paragraph from the *Robinson Crusoe* extract often consists of a long complex sentence. For example see lines 39-46. Such a sentence usually only ever appears in writing. It would sound very strange if anybody spoke like this.

On the other hand, in *Talking in Whispers*, it is easy to imagine people speaking some of the paragraphs. The writer has tried to give the impression of speech. It is not actual speech but the writer knows enough of what spontaneous speech sounds like to be able to imitate it for his story.

9 **Think about what you know about real speech. Contrast the imitation of it in *Talking in Whispers* with the language and grammar of *Robinson Crusoe*.**

[10 marks – Q9]

Part 6   Word Level: Spelling

These questions assess your ability to explain spelling patterns, show understanding of word formation and spell correctly.

Read this passage about diet in hospitals.

All hospital dieticians agree that correct diet is of great <u>importance</u> in making treatment a <u>success</u>. It is a physiological <u>necessity</u> and has important <u>psychologica</u>l benefits. Careful consideration of the <u>quality</u> and quantity of food and drink will help on the road to <u>complete</u> recovery <u>whether</u> fighting disease or recovering from surgery.

Now look at the underlined words and answer the questions which follow.

10 Look at the noun 'importance'.

Write the adjective formed from the same stem.

[1 mark – Q10]

Grammar section

GRAMMAR SECTION

MARKS

11 *Look at the words 'necessity' and 'quality'.*

   a Write down the plural of one of these words.

[1] Q11a

   b Explain what spelling pattern the formation of this plural follows.

[1] Q11b

12 *Look at the word 'psychological'. This word begins with the prefix, 'psycho-'.*

Explain what the prefix 'psycho-' means. Then write down another word (but not 'psychology') which begins with the prefix 'psycho-' or 'psych-'.

[2] Q12

13 *Look at the noun 'success'.*

   a Write down the plural of 'success'.

[1] Q13a

   b Write down an adjective formed from 'success'.

[1] Q13b

14 *Look at the verb 'complete'.*

Write down a noun formed from the same stem.

[1] Q14

15 *Look at the word 'whether'.*

Write down a common homophone (a word which sounds the same but is spelled differently) for this word and use it correctly in a sentence.

[1] Q15

16 Write down another pair of homophones and explain what each word in the pair means. You can base this pair on a word from the passage or choose other words.

[1] Q16

54

Grammar section Answers

Part 1 Sentence Level

1 The four connectives are:
- when
- and
- which
- about

One mark for each correct answer: 4 marks
Total 4 marks

2 The five simple sentences are:
- I came down from my appartment in the tree.
- I look'd about me again.
- The first thing I found was the boat.
- The boat lay as the wind and sea had tossed her up upon the land.
- The boat was about two miles on my right hand.

One mark for each correct answer: 5 marks
Total 5 marks

3 Possible reasons are:
- 18th century writers wrote much longer sentences than writers usually do today.
- Robinson Crusoe has more time to explore his surroundings than Andres has in ***Talking in Whispers***.
- James Watson uses shorter sentences in ***Talking in Whispers*** to create a sense of danger and urgency.
- The writer of Robinson Crusoe wants his reader to be able to imagine Crusoe's situation and so includes lots of detail.

Two marks each for any two of the above reasons: 4 marks
Total 4 marks

4 There are **seven** phrases in this extract:
- in a word
- about me
- but a knife
- a tobacco-pipe
- a little tobacco
- in a box
- all my provision

Award one mark for each phrase identified up to a total of six: 6 marks
Total 6 marks

55

Grammar section Answers

Part 2 Word Level: Spelling

5   Here are the modern spellings of the words in bold type.
 a   wrapped
 b   fir
 c   die
 d   tide
 e   apartment
 f   hoped

Award one mark for each correct spelling: 6 marks
Total 6 marks

Part 3 Word Level: Parts of Speech

6   These are the correctly identified parts of speech:
 a   noun
 b   adverb
 c   adjective
 d   noun
 e   verb

Award two marks for each correct answer: 10 marks
Total 10 marks

Part 4 Word Level: Language Changes

7   Here you have been asked to rewrite the language examples from **Robinson Crusoe** as they might be written today. If your answers are similar to the ones below then award yourself the marks.
 a   'I was the only one saved' *or*
     'I was the only survivor'
 b   'I looked at the stranded ship' *or*
     'I glanced at the ship' *or*
     'I looked towards the ship'
 c   'Night was falling' *or*
     'It was nearly night' *or*
     'It was going dark'
 d   'tired out' *or*
     'I was very tired' *or*
     'exhausted'
 e   'I walked as far as I could along the shore'

Award two marks for each answer: 10 marks
Total 10 marks

Grammar section Answers

Part 5 Text Level

There are two questions in this section and each is worth 10 marks.

8   This question expects you to point out some of the differences in the way the two extracts are written. If you have five contrasts that are similar to the ones that follow then give yourself two marks for each. Remember any **five** of the following differences will give you the full 10 marks for this question.
- There are six paragraphs in the **Robinson Crusoe** extract and more than thirty in **Talking in Whispers**. Short paragraphs give a sense of urgency and danger. Long paragraphs give the impression of time moving slowly.
- Lots of dangerous things happen suddenly in **Talking in Whispers**. So there are lots of short sentences and even one-word paragraphs. There are very few events in the **Robinson Crusoe** extract although there is plenty of detail about what he thought and noticed. His thoughts are complicated and detailed and so are the sentences that tell the reader what he is thinking. Sometimes one long sentence makes one long paragraph.
- Phrases in **Robinson Crusoe** are used for lists. Phrases in **Talking in Whispers** are used to hurry the action forward and to introduce extra excitement. For example, 'An American.' in line 17.
- The language in **Robinson Crusoe** is difficult. The language in **Talking in Whispers** is simpler. For example, 'After I had solac'd my mind with the comfortable part of my condition,' from **Robinson Crusoe** compared with, 'Andres felt a thrill of hope' from **Talking in Whispers.** Both sentences refer to hope but one sentence is much simpler. The difference is caused by the way writing styles have changed over time.
- Robinson Crusoe is by himself. Andres is part of a packed crowd. He can only notice bits and pieces of what happens. Robinson Crusoe, however, is entirely alone in this extract and can leisurely notice as much as he wants to. The language structures of the two passages reinforce this difference in their two situations.

Award two marks for each similar contrast: 10 marks
Total 10 marks

9   What are the features of spontaneous or 'real' speech? Which of these features does the **Talking in Whispers** extract imitate? Why do you think no one speaks (although they may write) in the style of the **Robinson Crusoe** extract?

If your answer contains five similar points to the ones below, award yourself the full 10 marks.
- There are incomplete sentences in **Talking in Whispers**. For example, 'But –'. This is an incomplete and interrupted sentence. This is a feature of real speech.
- 'Permiso! Give us passage, folks – it's for a good cause.' Informal expressions and sudden changes of subject are also features of real speech.
- Short sentences that rely on the person being present to make proper sense. For example, in **Talking in Whispers**, 'That's my friend – the tall one.' A real speaker could point if there was any doubt which person was being referred to. A writer has to use description. Here there is a bit of both because it is an imitation of real speech.
- Repetition as in 'Please – please let me through...' is a feature of real speech in **Talking in Whispers**.

Robinson Crusoe has **no** features of real or spontaneous speech. There are plenty of structures that are usually only found in writing. Some of these are:
- Long complex sentences with subordinate clauses.

Grammar section Answers

- Long compound sentences using three or four connectives with words missed but understood. See the example that was used in question 2 in the Sentence Level Section on page 48. You had to write out the five simple sentences that made up one sentence; for two of your simple sentences you had to add the words 'the boat' that were understood in the original, long sentence.
- Long complicated single sentence paragraphs that can be re-read if necessary. It is impossible to do this in real speech so people do not speak in this style.

Award two marks for each similar contrast: 10 marks
Total 10 marks

Part 6 Word Level: Spellings

10   important

1 mark
Total 1 mark

11a equalities *or* necessities *1 mark*

  b When 'y' follows a consonant, change the 'y' to 'i' before adding the plural ending '-es'.

1 mark
Total 2 marks

12a Answer should include 'psycho' means 'mind' or a similar explanation.

1 mark

  b There are many appropriate words, e.g. psychiatry/psychopath, psychedelic, etc. (Check spelling and other alternatives in a dictionary.)

1 mark
Total 2 marks

13a successes

1 mark

  b successful
     (Note: 'successive' is not formed from 'success'.)

1 mark
Total 2 marks

14   completion *or* completeness *or* completedness

1 mark
Total 1 mark

15   The word 'weather' and a sentence or phrase which shows understanding of its meaning.

1 mark
Total 1 mark

16   An example from the passage is the word 'road' (rode). You could use any other pair of homophones with an accurate explanation of their meanings. (Check spellings and meanings in a dictionary).

1 mark
Total 1 mark

Grammar section
Determining your level

MARKING GRID

GRAMMAR SECTION *Pages 48–54*

		Marks available	Marks scored
Part 1	Sentence Level	19	
Part 2	Word Level: Spelling	6	
Part 3	Word Level: Parts of Speech	10	
Part 4	Word Level: Language Changes	10	
Part 5	Text Level	20	
Part 6	Word Level: Spelling	10	
Total		**75**	

FINDING YOUR LEVEL

When you have marked this section, enter the marks you scored for each part on the Marking Grid above. Then add them up. Using your total score, look at the charts below to determine your level.

Level 4 or below	Level 5	Level 6	Level 7	Above Level 7
1–15	16–30	31–45	46–60	61–75

English Booklet

Talking in Whispers

This is part of a novel by James Watson. It is set in Chile in the 1970s during the rule of General Pinochet and his army. Political prisoners are being taken by the army* to the National Stadium. Andres, a teenage boy, is searching for his friend, Braulio.

Andres stayed clear of the crowd. He watched the arrival of another truck. The soldiers did not care if their brutality was witnessed by hundreds of people. Those prisoners who hesitated as they climbed from the truck were hastened on their way with rifle butts.
　'Move, scum!'
　Suddenly Andres broke forward, seeking a gap in the wall of people. 'Braulio!' There was no doubt. His friend had jumped from the truck. He was handcuffed. 'Braulio!' Andres fought to get through the crowd.
　Braulio Altuna stood a head taller than the other prisoners in line. A stream of blood had congealed down one side of his face.
　Andres forgot his own danger. He must get to Braulio, at the very least let him know that somebody had proof that he was alive.
　'Please – please let me through – my friend is out there!' Andres looked to be having no luck in prising a way through the crowd when he spotted a tall man in a white mack, making better progress.
　'Permiso! Give us a passage, folks – it's for a good cause.'
　An American.
　Andres tucked himself in behind the man, burly, fair-haired, with out-thrust arm, shoving a sideways path towards the truck and the gates of the stadium.
　Andres got so close to the American that he could have picked his pocket. He glanced down and saw that the man was holding something behind him, wrapped in a carrier bag.
　For an instant, Andres decided that the American had a gun. Yet the compulsion to make contact with Braulio proved greater than Andres' fear that he might have landed himself in a shoot-out.
　The object which the American slipped from the carrier bag had indeed many more shots than a pistol. A camera! He's a pressman. Andres felt a thrill of hope. Here comes the American cavalry! He was right behind the pressman. He shouted in Spanish:
　'Give him room!' And then in a low voice only audible to the American, 'The world's got to know what's happening here.'
　'You bet it has.' The pressman took Andres in in one friendly – even grateful – glance. They were comrades. Together they breasted a way through the crowd.
　'That's my friend – the tall one.'
　The last prisoners were being driven from the truck. One was not fast enough to please his guards. He was hurt, hobbling, gripping his side in pain.
　'Step on it, you red scab!'
　The American's camera was in the air. A rifle butt swung against the stumbling prisoner.
　Click-whirr, click-whirr – the scene was banked, recorded.
　Braulio had turned, stepping out of line. He protested at the guard's action and immediately drew soldiers round him like wasps to honey.
　Click-whirr, click-whirr. The toppling of Braulio was captured. Here was evidence for the time when villainy would be brought to justice.

* The 'Black Berets'

Yet here also was terrible danger. The American photographer had himself been snapped by the eye of the officer commanding the troops. 'Christ. They've spotted me!' He lowered his camera swiftly below the shoulders of the crowd. He shifted, half-face towards Andres. He seemed paralysed by fear.

The American pushed the camera into Andres' hand. 'Take this – I'm finished.'

'But –'

'I beg you. The film in that camera…'

The officer and his men were clubbing a passage through the crowd towards the American. Andres ducked the camera through the open zip of his jacket. 'Who shall I say?' He was being carried away from the pressman by the retreat of the crowd.

'Chailey – Don Chailey!' He yelled the name of his newspaper too but the words did not carry to Andres who found himself squeezed step by step away from the oncoming troops.

The crowd had saved Andres. It had no power to delay sentence upon the American. The soldiers were all round him. Momentarily his fair hair could be seen between their helmets. Then his arms went up above his head. He folded under a rampage of blows. He was hammered to the ground. He was kicked in the body, in the head, his hands stamped upon, his ribs skewered with iron-shod boots.

And now they were searching for his camera. They were demanding answers from the crowd, accusing them, turning their violence upon the innocent, frisking everyone who could have been within orbit of the American.

For an eternal second, Andres stood and watched. He saw Don Chailey dragged towards the stadium entrance. He saw him flung into one of the turnstiles.

Andres trembled as if touched by an electrified fence. Till now, he had wandered helplessly, insignificant. Soaked to the skin, he had arrived at the final blank wall and closed gate. His brain, his heart, his passionate resolve – they were nothing in the face of the Junta's untouchable strength.

But now… A chance in a million, an encounter lasting no longer than two minutes, had changed everything. He was in possession of something the military would like to get their hands on – proof of their brutality. What's more, Andres was witness to what the Black Berets had done to a citizen of the United States of America.

The Americans don't pour millions of dollars into Chile for us to beat up their newspapermen. Andres was at the street corner, poised for flight. All at once he had a purpose, a direction, a next step. He tapped the camera reverently. Somehow I must contact the Resistance. What's in this camera might be just as valuable as bullets.

English Booklet

news take action donate buy get involved search contact
About Oxfam Emergencies Development Campaigns Policy Fair Trade Shops Publications Kids&schools

educationow

Tanzania - no longer free

After Independence, Tanzania prided itself on the introduction of free primary education for all. Low government revenues, high debt repayments, and the constraints required by the IMF and World Bank have since seen schools starved of cash.

Currently the government spends twice as much per capita on debt repayments as on education, and four times as much on primary education. Pressures from rich governments and international institutions to introduce cost recovery have seen the introduction and increase of fees and other charges levied on all parents.

More than two million Tanzanian children are not in school, and illiteracy is rising at 2 per cent a year. In some schools there is one desk for every 38 pupils; one textbook for every four children; one toilet for every 89 pupils. Classrooms crumble unless parents can fund their rebuilding. Teachers have been left demoralised by falling salaries, worsening conditions, and increasing class sizes.

In Kenya and Uganda, if parents cannot pay the fees, the children go home. But primary schooling remains compulsory under Tanzania's Education Act. Head teachers and education department staff are under increasing pressure to act as debt collectors, they become preoccupied with cost recovery, harassing parents and sending children home until payments are made.

In fact, many parents simply cannot pay the charges. In Shinyanga District's rural schools, for example, only 36 per cent of fees were collected successfully in 1997. The combination of fees and other charges is making it impossible for parents to send all their children to primary school.

Oxfam has estimated that in Tanzania $100 million could be generated by debt relief. Half of this amount would pay for repairs to 10,000 classrooms, would provide safe water and sanitation to 5,000 primary schools, and would provide services to disadvantaged groups, including disabled people, school drop-outs, and illiterate adults.

http://www.oxfam.org.uk

English Booklet

A child's view

Regina is 12 years old. She lives in Nyabiyonza village in Karagwe District, where Oxfam has funded a brand-new brick school.

But Regina is an orphan, and her adoptive mother cannot afford to send her to the school this year. She is so keen to go that she won't admit that this is anything but a temporary setback.

photo: Geoff Sayer/Oxfam

"I haven't stopped. It's just that I haven't started this year. We don't have money for the school contributions, and I have no uniform. That's why I couldn't go."

A parent's view

Mwange Saidi lives in Shinyanga town. She earns the equivalent of 30p a day by selling tomatoes, root ginger, soap, and other small items from a stall outside her home.

Her two daughters, Ramdwa and Sada, often get sent home from Uhuru Primary School, because she can't afford to pay the school fees. The fees, uniforms, and books cost the equivalent of about £25 a year.

photo: Geoff Sayer/Oxfam

"It would be much easier for parents if the government would pay for primary education. I want my children to have an education. It's important for the girls, because it will help them to earn their own living and to take care of their family – like I do now. Education helps me to take care of my children, and to keep them healthy."

> <u>Debt is a major obstacle to education.</u>

> <u>Take action now</u> to demand debt relief

stories
> <u>Chemjor's story</u>
> Tanzania case study
> <u>Lisa Potts visits Vietnam</u>

educationnow
<u>take action</u>
<u>issues</u>
<u>stories</u>
<u>in-depth</u>

free internet access

http://www.oxfam.org.uk

Oxfam

English Booklet

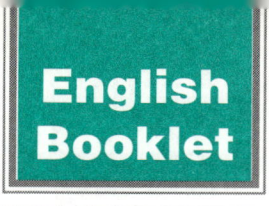

Henry V   Act 4 Scene 1 (extract)
Scene 1 The English Camp at Agincourt

Enter Pistol.
PISTOL	Qui va la?
KING HENRY	A friend.
PISTOL	Discuss unto me: art thou officer? Or art thou base, common and popular?
KING HENRY	I am a gentleman of a company.
PISTOL	Trail'st thou the puissant pike?
KING HENRY	Even so. What are you?
PISTOL	As good a gentleman as the emperor.
KING HENRY	Then you are a better than the king.
PISTOL	The king's a bawcock, and a heart of gold. A lad of life, an imp of fame; Of parents good, of fist most valiant: I kiss his dirty shoe, and from heart-string I love the lovely bully. What's thy name?
KING HENRY	Harry le Roy.
PISTOL	Le Roy! a Cornish name: art thou of Cornish crew?
KING HENRY	No, I am a Welshman.
PISTOL	Know'st thou Fluellen?
KING HENRY	Yes.
PISTOL	Tell him, I'll knock his lock about his pate Upon Saint Davy's day.
KING HENRY	Do not you wear your dagger in your cap that day, lest he knock that about yours.
PISTOL	Art thou his friend?
KING HENRY	And his kinsman too.
PISTOL	The figo for thee then!
KING HENRY	I thank you. God be with you!
PISTOL	My name is Pistol called.

Exit
KING HENRY	It sorts well with your fierceness.

Enter Fluellen and Gower, severally
GOWER	Captain Fluellen!
FLUELLEN	So! in the name of Jeshu Christ, speak lower. It is the greatest admiration in the universal world, when the true and aunchient prerogatifes and laws of the wars is not kept. If you would take the pains but to examine the wars of Pompey the Great, you shall find, I warrant you, that there is no tiddle taddle nor pibble pabble in Pompey's camp; I warrant you, you shall find the ceremonies of the wars, and the cares of it, and the forms of it, and the sobriety of it, and the modesty of it, to be otherwise.
GOWER	Why, the enemy is loud; you hear him all night.
FLUELLEN	If the enemy is an ass and a fool and a prating coxcomb, is it meet, think you, that we should also, look you, be an ass and a fool and a prating coxcomb? in your own conscience now?
GOWER	I will speak lower.
FLUELLEN	I pray you and peseech you that you will.

Exeunt Gower and Fluellen
KING HENRY	Though it appear a little out of fashion, There is much care and valour in this Welshman.

Enter three soldiers, John Bates, Alexander Court and Michael Williams
COURT	Brother John Bates, is not that the morning which breaks yonder?
BATES	I think it be; but we have no great cause to desire the approach of day.
WILLIAMS	We see yonder the beginning of the day, but I think we shall never see the end of it. Who goes there?
KING HENRY	A friend.
WILLIAMS	Under what captain serve you?
KING HENRY	Under Sir Thomas Erpingham.
WILLIAMS	A good old commander and a most kind gentleman; I pray you, what thinks he of our estate?

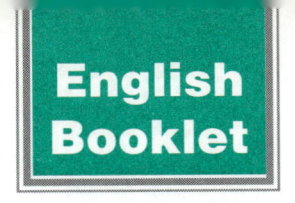

KING HENRY	Even as men wrecked upon a sand, that look, to be washed off the next tide.
BATES	He hath not told his thought to the king!
KING HENRY	No; nor it is not meet he should. For, though I speak it to you, I think the king is but a man, as I am; the violet smells to him as it doth to me; the element shows to him as it doth to me; all his senses have but human conditions: his ceremonies laid by, in his nakedness he appears but a man; and though his affections are higher mounted than ours, yet when they stoop, they stoop with the like wing. Therefore when he sees reason of fears, as we do, his fears, out of doubt, be of the same relish as ours are: yet, in reason, no man should possess him with any appearance of fear, lest he, by showing it should dishearten his army.
BATES	He may show what outward courage he will, but I believe, as cold a night as 'tis, he could wish himself in Thames up to the neck, and so I would be were, and I by him, at all adventures, so we were quit here.
KING HENRY	By my troth, I will speak my conscience of the king; I think he would not wish himself any where but where he is.
BATES	Then I would he were here alone; so should he be sure to be ransomed, and a many poor men's lives saved.
KING HENRY	I dare say you love him not so ill to wish him here alone, howsoever you speak this to feel other men's minds. Methinks I could not die any where so contented as in the king's company, his cause being just and his quarrel honourable.
WILLIAMS	That's more than we know.
BATES	Ay, or more than we should seek after; for we know enough if we know we are the king's subjects. If his cause be wrong, our obedience to the king wipes the crime of it out of us.
WILLIAMS	But if the cause be not good, the king himself hath a heavy reckoning to make; when all those legs and arms and heads, chopped off in a battle, shall join together at the latter day, and cry all 'We died at such a place;' some swearing, some crying for a surgeon, some upon their wives left poor behind them, some upon the debts they owe, some upon their children rawly left. I am afeard there are few die well that die in a battle: for how can they charitably dispose of any thing when blood is their argument! Now, if these men do not die well, it will be a black matter for the king that led them to it, whom to disobey were against all proportion of subjection.
KING HENRY	So, if a son that is by his father sent about merchandise do sinfully miscarry upon the sea, the imputation of his wickedness, by your rule, should be imposed upon his father that sent him: or if a servant, under his master's command transporting a sum of money, be assailed by robbers and die in many irreconciled iniquities, you may call the business of the master the author of the servant's damnation. But this is not so: the king is not bound to answer the particular ending of his soldiers, the father of his son nor the master of his servant; for they purpose not their death when they purpose their services. Besides there is no king, be his cause never so spotless if it come to the arbitrament of swords, can try it out with all unspotted soldiers. Some, peradventure, have on them the guilt of premeditated and contrived murder; some, of beguiling virgins with the broken seals of perjury; some, making the wars their bulwark, that have before gored the gentle bosom of peace with pillage and robbery. Now, if these men have defeated the law and outrun native punishment, though they can outstrip men, they have no wings to fly from God: war is his beadle, war is his vengeance; so that here men are punished for before-breach of the king's laws in now the king's quarrel: where they feared the death they have borne life away, and where they would be safe they perish. Then, if they die unprovided, no more is the king guilty of their damnation than he was before guilty of those impieties for the which they are now visited. Every subject's duty is the king's; but every subject's soul is his own. Therefore should every soldier in the wars do as every sick man in his bed, wash every mote out of his conscience; and dying so, death is to him advantage; or not dying, the time was blessedly lost wherein such preparation was gained: and in him that escapes, it were not sin to think that, making God so free an offer, He let him outlive that day to see His greatness, and to teach others how they should prepare.

WILLIAMS	'Tis certain, every man that dies ill, the ill upon his own head; the king is not to answer it.
BATES	I do not desire he should answer for me; and yet I determine to fight lustily for him.
KING HENRY	I myself heard the king say he would not be ransomed.
WILLIAMS	Ay, he said so, to make us fight cheerfully; but when our threats are cut he may be ransomed, and we ne'er the wiser.
KING HENRY	If I live to see it, I will never trust his word after.
WILLIAMS	You pay him then. That's a perilous shot out of an elder-gun that a poor and private displeasure can do against a monarch. You may as well go about to turn the sun to ice with fanning in his face with a peacock's feather. You'll never trust his word after! come, 'tis a foolish saying.
KING HENRY	Your reproof is something too round; I should be angry with you if the time were convenient.
WILLIAMS	Let it be a quarrel between us, if you live.
KING HENRY	I embrace it.
WILLIAMS	How shall I know thee again?
KING HENRY	Give me any gage of thine, and I will wear it in my bonnet: then, if ever thou darest acknowledge it, I will make it my quarrel.
WILLIAMS	Here's my glove: give me another of thine.
KING HENRY	There.
WILLIAMS	This will I also wear in my cap: if ever thou come to me and say after to-morrow, 'This is my glove,' by this hand I will take thee a box on the ear.
KING HENRY	If ever I live to see it, I will challenge it.
WILLIAMS	Thou darest as well be hanged.
KING HENRY	Well, I will do it, though I take thou in the king's company.
WILLIAMS	Keep thy word: fare thee well.
BATES	Be friends, you English fools, be friends: we have French quarrels enow, if you could tell how to reckon.
KING HENRY	Indeed, the French may lay twenty French crowns to one, they will beat us; for they bear them on their shoulders: but it is no English treason to cut French crowns, and to-morrow the king himself will be a clipper.

Exeunt Soldiers

Upon the king! let us our lives, our souls,
Our debts, our careful wives,
Our children, and our sins lay on the king!
We must bear all. O hard condition!
Twin-born with greatness, subject to the breath
Of every fool, whose sense no more can feel
But his own wringing. What infinite heart's ease
Must kings neglect that private men enjoy!
And what have kings that privates have not too,
Save ceremony, save general ceremony?
And what art thou, thou idol ceremony?
What kind of god art thou, that suffer'st more
Of mortal griefs than do thy worshippers?
What are thy rents? what are thy comings-in?
O ceremony! show me but thy worth:
What is thy soul of adoration?
Art thou ought else but place, degree and form,
Creating awe and fear in other men?
Wherein thou art loss happy, being fear'd,
Than they in fearing.
What drink'st thou oft, instead of homage sweet,
But poison'd flattery? O! be sick, great greatness,
And bid thy ceremony give thee cure.
Think'st thou the fiery fever will go out
With titles blown from adulation
Will it give place to flexure and low-bending?
Canst thou, when thou command'st the beggar's knee,
Command the health of it? No, thou proud dream,
That play'st so subtly with a king's repose;
I am a king that find thee; and I know
'Tis not the balm, the sceptre and the ball,
The sword, the mace, the crown imperial,
The intertissued robe of gold and pearl,
The farced title running 'fore the king,
The throne he sits on, nor the tide of pomp
That beats upon the high shore of this world,
No, not all these, thrice-gorgeous ceremony,
Not all these, laid in bed majestical,
Can sleep so soundly as the wretched slave,
Who with a body fill'd and vacant mind
Gets him to rest, cramm'd with distressful bread;
Never sees horrid night, the child of hell,
But, like a lackey, from the rise to set
Sweats in the eye of Phoebus, and all night.
Sleeps in Elysium; next day after dawn,
Doth rise and help Hyperion to his horse,
And follows so the ever-running year
With profitable labour to his grave:
And, but for ceremony, such a wretch,
Winding up days with toil and nights with sleep,
Had the fore-hand and vantage of a king.
The slave, a member of the country's peace,
Enjoys it; but in gross brain little wots
What watch the king keeps to maintain the peace,
Whose hours the peasant best advantages.

Exeunt

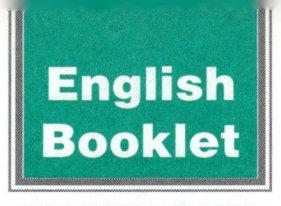

Macbeth
Act 1 Scene 7
Macbeth's castle   Near the Great Hall

Hautboys. Torches. Enter a butler and many servants with dishes and service over the stage. Then enter MACBETH.

MACBETH	If it were done when 'tis done, then 'twere well	
	It were done quickly. If th'assassination	
	Could trammel up the consequence and catch	
	With his surcease, success, that but this blow	
	Might be the be-all and the end-all – here,	5
	But here, upon this bank and shoal of time,	
	We'd jump the life to come. But in these cases,	
	We still have judgement here that we but teach	
	Bloody instructions, which being taught, return	
	To plague th'inventor. This even-handed justice	10
	Commends th'ingredience of our poisoned chalice	
	To our own lips. He's here in double trust:	
	First, as I am his kinsman and his subject,	
	Strong both against the deed; then, as his host,	
	Who should against his murderer shut the door,	15
	Not bear the knife myself. Besides, this Duncan	
	Hath borne his faculties so meek, hath been	
	So clear in his great office, that his virtues	
	Will plead like angels, trumpet-tongued against	
	The deep damnation of his taking-off.	20
	And pity, like a naked newborn babe	
	Striding the blast, or heaven's cherubin horsed	
	Upon the sightless couriers of the air,	
	Shall blow the horrid deed in every eye,	
	That tears shall drown the wind. I have no spur	25
	To prick the sides of my intent, but only	
	Vaulting ambition which o'erleaps itself	
	And falls on th'other –	

Enter LADY [MACBETH]

	How now? What news?	
LADY MACBETH	He has almost supped. Why have you left the chamber?	
MACBETH	Hath he asked for me?	
LADY MACBETH	Know you not he has?	30
MACBETH	We will proceed no further in this business.	
	He hath honoured me of late, and I have bought	
	Golden opinions from all sorts of people,	
	Which would be worn now in their newest gloss,	
	Not cast aside so soon.	
LADY MACBETH	Was the hope drunk	35
	Wherein you dressed yourself? Hath it slept since?	
	And wakes it now to look so green and pale	
	At what it did so freely? From this time,	

	Such I account thy love. Art thou afeard	
	To be the same in thine own act and valour,	40
	As thou art in desire? Wouldst thou have that	
	Which thou esteem'st the ornament of life,	
	And live a coward in thine own esteem,	
	Letting 'I dare not' wait upon 'I would',	
	Like the poor cat i'th'adage?	
MACBETH	Prithee, peace.	45
	I dare do all that may become a man;	
	Who dares do more is none.	
LADY MACBETH	What beast was't then	
	That made you break this enterprise to me?	
	When you durst do it, then you were a man.	
	And to be more than what you were, you would	50
	Be so much more the man. Nor time, nor place	
	Did then adhere, and yet you would make both.	
	They have made themselves and their fitness now	
	Does unmake you. I have given suck and know	
	How tender 'tis to love the babe that milks me:	55
	I would, while it was smiling in my face,	
	Have plucked my nipple from his boneless gums	
	And dashed the brains out, had I so sworn	
	As you have done to this.	
MACBETH	If we should fail?	
LADY MACBETH	We fail?	
	But screw your courage to the sticking place,	60
	And we'll not fail. When Duncan is asleep,	
	Whereto the rather shall his day's hard journey	
	Soundly invite him, his two chamberlains	
	Will I with wine and wassail so convince	
	That memory, the warder of the brain,	65
	Shall be a fume, and the receipt of reason	
	A limbeck only. When in swinish sleep	
	Their drenched natures lies as in a death,	
	What cannot you and I perform upon	
	Th'unguarded Duncan? What not put upon	70
	His spongy officers, who shall bear the guilt	
	Of our great quell?	
MACBETH	Bring forth men-children only,	
	For thy undaunted mettle should compose	
	Nothing but males. Will it not be received,	
	When we have marked with blood those sleepy two	75
	Of his own chamber and used their very daggers,	
	That they have done't?	
LADY MACBETH	Who dares receive it other,	
	As we shall make our griefs and clamour roar	
	Upon his death?	
MACBETH	I am settled and bend up	
	Each corporal agent to this terrible feat.	80
	Away, and mock the time with fairest show,	
	False face must hide what the false heart doth know.	
	Exeunt	

Twelfth Night
Act 1 Scene 5, Lines 136–253
Scene 5   A room in Olivia's house

OLIVIA	Give me my veil; come throw it o'er my face. We'll once more hear Orsino's embassy.	
	Enter VIOLA	
VIOLA	The honourable lady of the house, which is she?	
OLIVIA	Speak to me; I shall answer for her. Your will?	140
VIOLA	Most radiant, exquisite, and unmatchable beauty – I pray you tell me if this be the lady of the house, for I never saw her. I would be loath to cast away my speech: for besides that it is excellently well penned, I have taken great pains to con it. Good beauties, let me sustain no scorn; I am very comptible, even to the least sinister usage.	145
OLIVIA	Whence came you, sir?	
VIOLA	I can say little more than I have studied, and that question's out of my part. Good gentle one, give me modest assurance if you be the lady of the house, that I may proceed in my speech.	150
OLIVIA	Are you a comedian?	
VIOLA	No, my profound heart; and yet, by the very fangs of malice, I swear, I am not that I play. Are you the lady of the house?	
OLIVIA	If I do not usurp myself, I am.	
VIOLA	Most certain, if you are she, you do usurp yourself: for what is yours to bestow is not yours to reserve. But this is from my commission. I will on with my speech in your praise, and then show you the heart of my message.	155
OLIVIA	Come to what is important in't: I forgive you the praise.	
VIOLA	Alas, I took great pains to study it, and 'tis poetical.	160
OLIVIA	It is the more like to be feigned; I pray you keep it in. I heard you were saucy at my gates, and allowed your approach rather to wonder at you than to hear you. If you be not mad, be gone; if you have reason, be brief. 'Tis not that time of moon with me to make one in so skipping a dialogue.	165
MARIA	Will you hoist sail, sir? Here lies your way.	
VIOLA	No, good swabber, I am to hull here a little longer. Some mollification for your giant, sweet lady! Tell me your mind, I am a messenger.	
OLIVIA	Sure you have some hideous matter to deliver, when the courtesy of it is so fearful. Speak your office.	170
VIOLA	It alone concerns your ear. I bring no overture of war, no taxation of homage; I hold the olive in my hand; my words are as full of peace as matter.	
OLIVIA	Yet you began rudely. What are you? What would you?	175
VIOLA	The rudeness that hath appeared in me I learned from my entertainment. What I am, and what I would, are as secret as maidenhead: to your ears, divinity; to any other's profanation.	
OLIVIA	Give us the place alone; we will hear this divinity.	
	[*Exeunt Maria and Attendants*]	

	Now, sir, what is your text?	180
VIOLA	Most sweet lady –	
OLIVIA	A comfortable doctrine, and much may be said of it. Where lies your text?	
VIOLA	In Orsino's bosom.	
OLIVIA	In his bosom? In what chapter of his bosom?	185
VIOLA	To answer by the method, in the first of his heart.	
OLIVIA	O I have read it. It is heresy. Have you no more to say?	
VIOLA	Good madam, let me see your face.	
OLIVIA	Have you any commission from your lord to negotiate with my face? You are now out of your text, but we will draw the curtain and show you the picture. [*Unveiling*] Look you, sir, such a one I was this present. Is't not well done?	190
VIOLA	Excellently done, if God did all.	
OLIVIA	'Tis in grain, sir; 'twill endure wind and weather.	
VIOLA	'Tis beauty truly blent, whose red and white Nature's own sweet and cunning hand laid on. Lady, you are the cruell'st she alive, If you will lead these graces to the grave, And leave the world no copy.	195
OLIVIA	O sir, I will not be so hard-hearted: I will give out divers schedules of my beauty. It shall be inventoried and every particle and utensil labelled to my will, as, *item*, two lips, indifferent red; *item*, two grey eyes, with lids to them; *item*, one neck, one chin, and so forth. Were you sent hither to 'praise me?	200
VIOLA	I see you what you are. You are too proud; But if you were the devil, you are fair! My lord and master loves you. O such love Could be but recompensed, though you were crowned The nonpareil of beauty.	205
OLIVIA	How does he love me?	
VIOLA	With adorations, fertile tears, With groans that thunder love, with sighs of fire.	210
OLIVIA	Your lord does know my mind. I cannot love him. Yet I suppose him virtuous, know him noble, Of great estate, of fresh and stainless youth; In voices well divulged, free, learned, and valiant, And in dimension, and the shape of nature, A gracious person. But yet I cannot love him. He might have took his answer long ago.	215
VIOLA	If I did love you in my master's flame, With such a suff'ring, such a deadly life, In your denial I would find no sense; I would not understand it.	220
OLIVIA	Why, what would you?	
VIOLA	Make me a willow cabin at your gate, And call upon my soul within the house; Write loyal cantons of contemned love, And sing them loud even in the dead of night; Hallow your name to the reverberate hills, And make the babbling gossip of the air Cry out 'Olivia!' O you should not rest Between the elements of air and earth	225 230

	But you should pity me!	
OLIVIA	You might do much.	
	What is your parentage?	
VIOLA	Above my fortunes, yet my state is well:	
	I am a gentleman.	
OLIVIA	Get you to your lord.	
	I cannot love him, Let him send no more –	235
	Unless (perchance) you come to me again,	
	To tell me how he takes it. Fare you well.	
	I thank you for your pains. Spend this for me.	
VIOLA	I am no fee'd post, lady; keep your purse;	
	My master, not myself, lacks recompense.	240
	Love makes his heart of flint that you shall love,	
	And let your fervour like my master's be	
	Placed in contempt. Farewell, fair cruelty. *Exit*	
OLIVIA	'What is your parentage?'	
	'Above my fortunes, yet my state is well:	245
	I am a gentleman.' I'll be sworn thou art;	
	Thy tongue, thy face, thy limbs, actions, and spirit	
	Do give thee five-fold blazon. Not too fast! Soft, soft!	
	Unless the master were the man – How now?	
	Even so quickly may one catch the plague?	250
	Methinks I feel this youth's perfections	
	With an invisible and subtle stealth	
	To creep in at mine eyes. Well, let it be.	

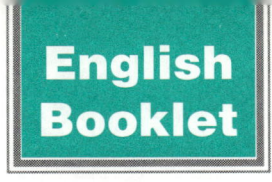

Robinson Crusoe

This is part of the story by Daniel Defoe about a shipwrecked sailor. It was first published in 1719. Robinson Crusoe is the only survivor and has struggled to the shore.

    I walk'd about on the shore, lifting up my hands, and my whole being, as may say, wrapt up in the contemplation of my deliverance, making a thousand gestures and motions which I cannot describe, reflecting upon all my comrades that were drown'd, and that there should not be one soul sav'd but my self; for, as for them, I never saw them afterwards, or any sign of them, except three of their hats, one cap, and two shoes that were not fellows.

    I cast my eyes to the stranded vessel, when the breach and froth of the sea being so big, I could hardly see it, it lay so far off, and considered Lord! how was it possible I could get on shore?

    After I had solac'd my mind with the comfortable part of my condition, I began to look round me to see what kind of place I was in, and what was next to be done, and I soon found my comforts abate, and that in a word I had a dreadful deliverance: for I was wet, had no clothes to shift me, nor any thing either to eat or drink to comfort me, neither did I see any prospect before me, but that of perishing with hunger, or being devour'd by wild beasts; and that which was particularly afflicting to me was that I had no weapon either to hunt and kill any creature for my sustenance, or to defend my self against any other creature that might desire to kill me for theirs. In a word, I had nothing about me but a knife, a tobacco-pipe, and a little tobacco in a box; this was all my provision, and this threw me into terrible agonies of mind, that for a while I ran about like a mad-man. Night coming upon me, I began with a heavy heart to consider what would be my lot if there were any ravenous beasts in that country, seeing at night they always come abroad for their prey.

    All the remedy that offer'd to my thoughts at that time was to get up into a thick bushy tree like a firr, but thorny, which grew near me, and where I resolv'd to sit all night, and consider the next day what death I should dye, for as yet I saw no prospect of life; I walk'd about a furlong from the shore, to see if I could find any fresh water to drink, which I did, to my great joy; and having drunk and put a little tobacco in my mouth to prevent hunger, I went to the tree, and getting up into it, endeavour'd to place my self so, as that if I should sleep I might not fall; and having cut me a short stick, like a truncheon, for my defence, I took up my lodging, and having been excessively fatigu'd, I fell fast asleep and slept as comfortably as, I believe, few could have done in my condition, and found my self the most refresh'd with it that I think I ever was on such an occasion.

When I wak'd it was broad day, the weather clear, and the storm abated, so that the sea did not rage and swell as before: but that which surpris'd me most was that the ship was lifted off in the night from the sand where she lay, by the swelling of the tyde, and was driven up almost as far as the rock which I first mention'd, where I had been so bruis'd by the dashing me against it; this being within about a mile from the shore where I was, and the ship seeming to stand upright still, I wish'd my self on board, that, at least, I might save some necessary things for my use. When I came down from my appartment in the tree, I look'd about me again, and the first thing I found was the boat, which lay as the wind and the sea had toss'd her up upon the land, about two miles on my right hand. I walk'd as far as I could upon the shore to have got to her, but found a neck or inlet of water between me and the boat, which was about half a mile broad, so I came back for the present, being more intent upon getting at the ship, where I hop'd to find something for my present subsistence.